# TRAVELLING LIGHT

# TRAVELLING LIGHT

*Christian Perspectives on Pilgrimage and Pluralism*

**William B. McClain**

**Friendship Press • New York**

Editorial Offices: 475 Riverside Drive, New York, NY 10115
Distribution Offices: P.O. Box 37844, Cincinnati, OH 45237

# DEDICATION

*To Jo Ann, Bobby and David*

# CONTENTS

# PREFACE

This book is about identity—the loss of it, the search for it, the recovery of it and the efforts involved in appreciating it—and about pluralism, which acknowledges, appreciates and nourishes the identity of persons and groups.

Persons who know who they are cannot be defined by others. Persons who know their names will not answer to other names they are called. Persons who are aware of their history and identity will not permit others to determine who they are or where they are going. Communities of persons with a sense of calling and an awareness of purpose will not allow others to speak for them nor judge their reason for being. But persons in a prodigal condition will answer to names that are not theirs, respond to calls and agendas set by others, and will spend their lives as "imaginary" people.

Prejudice, racism, sexism, cultural arrogance and nativism have stolen the identity of millions of people in this country and around the world. These negative "-isms" have tyrannized many for hundreds of years and cruelly twisted and warped the inner contours of their minds. Efforts toward liberation from negative "-isms" are yielding a positive choice: to be oneself and share in the riches of the human family. Pluralism asks that we allow others to be themselves without paying a dreadful price, and that we be ourselves without arrogant egotism, so that we can have the experience of truly loving other human beings.

There are, of course, some risks and dilemmas. This book attempts to look at some of the risks, at some of the rewards and at some of the requirements for the realization of genuine pluralism.

Prejudice and racism are still alive. To post an obituary notice now would be to misread the face of the clock of history. We have yet to find the instrument with which to strike the fatal blow. But we do know where it must land.

Meanwhile, as Christians, we still have to answer the question which Kelly Miller, a black sociologist and the Dean of Howard

University, asked more than seventy years ago: "What power is there in Christianity to wean men from their racial prejudice?" He was not being cynical. He was dead serious. He believed then that Christianity had, somewhere in its heart, the ability to transform sinful persons into redeeming instruments of God's purpose.

I believe that, too. That may be naive, but I still believe it. I believe that the Christian faith can join other faiths and ideologies as partners in a pluralism that liberates persons from indifference and ignorance, arrogance and selfishness and assists them in searching for and finding values and lifestyles that are not oppressive but just, that respect the right of individuals to be who they are because of Whose they are, and that can establish a global community in which dignity, justice and freedom are their uncontradicted and undisputed gifts at birth. This means following God in a winding pilgrimage of faithfulness: often not sure where it leads or whom we will encounter, but following obediently, travelling light—not taking much baggage with us—because God is on the way to establish a world in which every person can have bread with dignity, peace with justice, liberation with power and life with wholeness.

The chapters that follow are an effort to look at where we have been, where we are and who we have to be on that road. Thank God Paul won the argument with Peter at Antioch and the Council of Jerusalem ruled in favor of cultural pluralism!

# 1

# STRANGERS AT HOME

There is a Chinese proverb that says: "Only those who have washed their eyes with bitter water can see clearly." The history of ethnic minorities in the United States is the story of those whose eyes have been washed with bitter water, those who have "come over a way that with tears has been watered," and those who have trod the "Trail of Tears." This experience of ethnic oppression has been shared by Native Americans, black Americans, Asian-Americans and Hispanic-Americans—all have been treated as strangers at home. Nor has the Canadian experience been significantly different, for Canada, too, continues to experience the strains of domination and alienation among its factions as it struggles as a nation for its place and its identity in tomorrow's world.

A new understanding of history is the beginning of a change in perspective. It is only when history, with new agony and new insight, is pondered—where there is a creative brooding over the past and the present in search of meaning, form and perhaps hope—that a perception of what is possible can be clearly seen. It is this ancient lesson, rediscovered by black Americans through painful experience, shared by other minorities, that has led our ethnic minorities to address the basic problem, i.e., the ideological role that racism, prejudice and separatism play in the culture of the North American Christian community.

The roots of alienation and racism lie deep within the history of Western civilization. For almost two thousand years the Christian church has been dominated by a concept of God created in the image of the white man—a deity with the attributes of Caucasian idealization. The authority and power of Euro-American white men were equated with the authority and omnipotence of God.

In North America, Anglo-American culture, values, institutions and ideals have persisted as the norm. Condescension, paternalism and racism have been the inevitable consequent attitudes toward ethnic minorities. The religious basis of the ideology of the Christian West and much of the oppression of ethnic minorities are firmly rooted in white domination in all areas of faith and life. Ethnic oppression, racism, exclusion, nativist bigotry, exploitation, confinement and even massacre comprise the bitter story of our ethnic minorities.

## What Happened to Ethnic Groups: Ethnic Oppression

*Native Americans*. After crossing the frozen seas of the Bering Strait during the Ice Age 20,000 years ago, the first Americans became natives to this soil. Proud people that they were, they lived abundantly at home in the whole rich North American continent, until the white man came and made them strangers at home. Their land was taken, their "removal" became the federal policy, and this forced removal westward became what the Cherokees call "The Trail of Tears." The loss of their land was a loss of something of themselves and their identity as well. For, as Chief Seattle put it: "The shining water that moves in the streams and rivers is not just water but the blood of our ancestors. . . . Every shining pine needle, every sandy shore, every mist in the dark woods is holy in the memory of and experience of my people. The sap which courses through the trees carries the memory of the Red man."[1]

The early white settlers justified the extinction of the Native Americans on spurious theological grounds. They considered the gradual disappearance of the American Indians the will of God manifested. As one Puritan divine explained it: "God cast out the heathen to make room for his people." Speaking to his constituency, who saw themselves as God's elect and the "chosen people" of a "New Israel," Thomas Jefferson declared in his second inaugural address, "God led our forefathers, as Israel of old," implying that America and her institutions had divine approval and sanction. The whole process of establishment and expansion was seen as a God-ordained action to replace an inferior race with a superior one. Even such a celebrated patriarch as Benjamin Franklin declared that rum was "the appointed means" of fulfilling "the design of Providence to extirpate these savages in order to make room for the cultivation of the earth."[2]

The new settlers in America treated the Native Americans as if they had no dreams of their own, and made them simply characters in the

Anglo-Saxon's dream—characters to be deprived of their inherent rights to have their culture understood and respected, to be deprived of their land and their livelihood and, often and ruthlessly, of their very lives.

The heritage of the Native American is the story of long-forgotten and broken treaties, desecration of burial grounds and the revisitation of violence and tragedy at Wounded Knee in the winter of 1973. It is indeed a "Trail of Tears," a "Trail of Broken Treaties" and a heritage of centuries of injustices that have made Native Americans strangers at home.

*Asian-Americans and Pacific-Americans.* The story of Asian-Americans and Pacific-Americans is the story of ethnic oppression. The use of the term "Asian" to refer to such a diverse group of ethnic families is itself a clue to the problem. While there are some cultural similarities, common problems and common hopes, all that the Chinese, Japanese, Koreans and Taiwanese share for certain is color and a history of ethnic oppression, myths and stereotypes in this country. Asian-Americans include a number of different ethnic families, each with its own language, history and culture. But none have been exempt from the insidious tentacles of racism and gross exploitation.

Senator Thomas Hart Benton expressed in 1846 the attitude of nineteenth-century American Anglo-Saxons and the theological justification for the treatment of Asians. According to him, the Anglo-Saxons and the Celts "had alone received the divine command, to subdue and replenish the earth, and they would become the reviver and the regenerator of the inferior and torpid yellow peoples."[3] Biblical imagery and theological language, muddied over with nineteenth-century racism, were expounded to justify the Americans' treatment of those yellow peoples who emigrated to these shores.

Although the Chinese arrived in America in 1848 in time for the California gold rush, they were allowed only to serve as indentured servants to the miners. The Foreign Miner's Tax Law of 1856 preventing the Chinese from panning for gold was the first among many laws passed to discriminate against the "Asian-Americans." In 1859, a law was passed excluding Chinese from the public schools in San Francisco. In 1870, the Naturalization Act excluded Chinese persons from citizenship and forbade Chinese workers, already settled here, to bring their wives and families into the country to join them. Anti-Chinese race riots in cities occurred between 1871 and

1885; often for weeks, mobs of white Americans looted, burned and murdered numerous Chinese without any fear of penalty from law enforcement agencies.

Because of racism, the Chinese were caricatured and feared as "strangers." The white majority projected its own hate and fears onto the Chinese as the "other." Governor Bingler of California charged them with being "contract coolies, avaricious, ignorant of moral obligations, incapable of being assimilated and dangerous to the welfare of the state."[4] A report from a special committee to study the Chinese in San Francisco in 1885 was even more vicious in its attack. The Special Committee of the Board of Supervisors concluded: "The beasts of the field, the vagrant dogs that the Poundmaster gathers upon the streets to put to death by drowning, are vastly better worthy of our commiseration than the whole Mongolian race when they seek to overrun our country and blast American welfare and progress with their miserable, contaminating presence."[5] The churches reflected this same attitude and saw them not only as strangers to be feared, but as "pagans" and "heathens" to be converted, forgetting the words in Chronicles: "For we are strangers before thee, and sojourners, as all our fathers were" (I Chron. 29:15).

Japanese-Americans suffered similar experiences of ethnic oppression. In 1906, the San Francisco School Board passed a resolution which segregated all Korean, Chinese and Japanese children into a separate Oriental Public School. The reason given was "for the purpose of relieving the congestion at present prevailing in our schools." But the real reason was given in the words that followed: "but also for the higher end that our children should not be placed in any position where their youthful impressions may be affected by association with pupils of the Mongolian race."[6] In 1942, Executive Order 9066 placed more than one hundred thousand Japanese-Americans in concentration camps. Even though most were United States citizens, they were treated as strangers at home.

The treatment of Canadian residents of Japanese background was not sharply different. For example:

A Canadian citizen of Japanese origin was given a day's notice by the Government to close up shop for a forced sale of all his properties. He and his family were torn from their West Coast home to an interior point where they would live in a work camp

14

for the duration of World War II. Many citizens were glad to see the "Japs" removed, especially perhaps for business reasons. Others simply clung to the notion that this was a necessary policy in wartime, even though no Japanese Canadians were discovered to be disloyal. Only a very few voices were raised in protest.[7]

The fastest growing Asian-American family is the Korean-American. There are more than 300,000 Koreans living in the United States in 1980, as opposed to 70,000 in 1970. Although these new Americans are not the victims of exclusionary legislation, they are nevertheless affected by discrimination and racism, despite statistical characteristics that make their acceptance into the society seem desirable. More than 60 percent of the Korean-Americans identify with the Christian church. More than a third of the Korean-American population is college-educated, a percentage higher than that for United States citizens as a whole. Three-fourths of the Korean immigrants held professional, technical and managerial jobs in Korea. Yet Korean-Americans are drastically unemployed and underemployed. Professional persons, such as ministers and teachers, are often forced to accept work as janitors and waitresses. Ministers who have unusual competence, gifts, graces and experience and, in some cases, advanced degrees from schools in Korea and America, are denied transfers and recognition of their ordination in this country. Language difficulties are a factor in some cases, but racism is a bigger factor.

*Black Americans.* Although the Reverend Samuel Purchas described the New World in 1614 as one where the religiously conceived notion of the unity of humankind could be actualized, that ideal was soon forgotten with the arrival of the first black slaves five years later. His words were beautiful and the concept stated in language reminiscent of the New Testament:

> ... the tawney Moore, blacke Negro, duskie Libyan, ash-coloured American, should with the white European become *one sheep fold,* under *one great Sheepheard,* till this *mortalitie* being swallowed up of Life, wee may all *be one, as he* and the father *are one* ... without any more distinction of Colour, Nation, Language, Sexe, Condition, all may bee *One* in him that is One, and *onely blessed for ever.*[8]

As Robert Bellah rightly observes in *The Broken Covenant*, however: "On the one hand being a Christian meant a deep commitment to the oneness of man; on the other it meant the right of Christian Europeans to enslave or destroy any who differed radically from them in belief, custom, and complexion."[9]

The black American experience has been one of enslavement, discrimination and dehumanization. Since 1619 and their landing at Jamestown, black Americans have been victims of racism and ethnic oppression. Brought to this country in chains and auctioned off as property, stripped of their names, language, religion, culture and heritage and denied citizenship, the black people's pilgrimage in America has truly been "a way that with tears has been watered."

Lynchings and hangings of black persons became a recreational activity for whites. The eve of holy days seems to have been the day for unholy beginnings. Organized on Christmas Eve, 1865, immediately after the Civil War, the Ku Klux Klan rode in hooded robes by night for many years as they lynched, thrashed, hanged, castrated, murdered and quartered black Americans like animals. When the organization, though not its mentality, became somewhat quiescent just after the turn of the century, William Joseph Simons, a Methodist minister in Atlanta, Georgia, infused new life into a reorganized Klan on a Thanksgiving Eve. He built an altar on Stone Mountain in Georgia, placed the American flag, the Bible and a sword there, and set fire to a wooden cross. The cross, symbol of freedom and liberation for recently freed black Christians and of hope for those still enslaved, became a source of terror and fear. This period was indeed, as Benjamin Brawley called it, "The Vale of Tears."

Black Americans continue to experience the effects of a ubiquitous racism. A formidable structure of discriminatory laws grew up in the South, creating barriers of racial segregation in almost every area of interracial contact. The North practiced *de facto* segregation. These laws of segregation were to remain in effect until well into the 1960's and the force of them still persists. Enduring slavery for 244 years and legal segregation for a century, black Americans are still strangers at home, victims of an ever more complex racism. Legal battles have been won. Protests and civil rights movements have yielded improved legislation. Yet, the emerging conflict over the redistribution of wealth and power and the struggle for black control over the institutions which affect the quality of black lives continues.

*Hispanic-Americans*. Hispanic-Americans are a pluralism in themselves. They are multiple groups bound together by a mixed cultural heritage and language. "The indelible marks of Spanish, Indian, and in some cases African cultures have merged through the years to create a culture that is neither Spanish, Indian nor African, but Spanish American."[10] The first Hispanic-Americans were an indigenous people—native to the territories acquired by the United States. Sadly, much of the land of these Hispanics in the Southwest was taken by force, the people murdered or evicted to release the land. The story of Mexican farm workers and the exploitation of their labor and their lives has been well documented by Cesar Chavez and other leaders and organizers of farm workers. There are other Hispanic-Americans: those from Puerto Rico, annexed as the result of the Spanish-American War; Cubans who fled Castro's regime; others from countries in Central and South America and the Caribbean.

Many shades of color are represented among the Hispanic-Americans and yet a common experience of ethnic oppression. Whether they are rural or urban, middle-class or poor, immigrant or indigenous, sunbaked or not, all have been segregated, exploited and paternalized by white America. Grave inequalities in housing, employment and education have resulted from exclusion and discrimination. Whether in the city *barrio* or the farms and fields, Hispanics have experienced ethnic oppression as a result of racism and cultural imperialism.

While these ethnic minorities differ in background, culture, language and history, all have suffered and continue to suffer beneath a debilitating racism in North American culture in which the religion of America has played a significant role—both in what has been done to ethnic minorities and in how they have responded.

## The Realities of Racism

The facts of racism are embarrassing. They have been presented again and again, until there are those who despair that "knowing the facts" will ever provide sufficient leverage for change. But only within a setting of fact may we hope to deal creatively with what now looms as the major crisis of North America.

## Racism and Economic Exploitation

The Native Americans suffered genocide, saw their lands stolen and their dignity dismissed as they were herded onto barren reservations in the name of progress, enterprise and eminent domain. The importation of slaves was designed to make money for slave traders and to simplify life for those who had the capital to purchase slave labor. Immigrant laborers were exploited through lower wages and higher prices, and "illegal aliens" today find themselves in the same situation, with virtually no recourse. This is the heritage of contemporary racism and prejudice. These continue to be the mechanisms for the exploitation of minorities today.

Exploitation is accomplished in many ways: denying access to desirable jobs, privileges, benefits and opportunities; offering lower wages, but higher prices, higher rents, more difficult credit terms and poorer living and working conditions; limiting employment opportunities to certain undesirable or "dead-end" jobs that minorities find themselves compelled to accept for lack of viable alternatives. A plethora of statistics provides supporting evidence of the effectiveness of these exploitative mechanisms.

For example, some authorities argue that minority median income is on the rise and therefore minorities are doing better. This is only partially true. Table 1 shows the *widening gap* between minority and white incomes—and dispels one illusion of progress. The disparity is worse than it was 10 years ago and it shows every indication of widening even more. Rising inflation and constant threats of recession will prevent minority groups from ever catching up and closing the gap. For every minority family whose economic prospects are improving, three or four others are locked into poverty with virtually no hope of escape.

## Table 1

Median Income/$1,000's

|            | 1960 | 1965 | 1970 | 1975 | 1976 | 1977 |
|------------|------|------|------|------|------|------|
| Total U.S. | 5.6  | 7.0  | 9.9  | 13.7 | 15.0 | 16.0 |
| White      | 5.8  | 7.3  | 10.2 | 14.3 | 15.5 | 16.7 |
| Other      | 3.2  | 4.0  | 6.5  | 9.3  | 9.8  | 10.1 |

Source: *1978 Statistical Abstract of the U.S.*

The employment—or unemployment—statistics in Table 2 show the same unfortunate trends with an interesting addition. In this case, where sex differences are taken into account, *white male* unemployment rates always fall below the median, while white women join minorities (though not to the same degree, by any means) on the unemployment rosters. Still, white unemployment is always lower than the total U.S. median. Again, the relative gap between whites and minorities continues to widen.

## Table 2

Unemployment (%)

|  | 1960 | 1965 | 1970 | 1975 | 1976 | 1977 |
|---|---|---|---|---|---|---|
| Total | 5.5 | 4.5 | 4.9 | 8.5 | 7.7 | 7.0 |
| White | 4.9 | 4.1 | 4.5 | 7.8 | 7.0 | 6.2 |
|   Male | 4.8 | 3.6 | 4.0 | 7.2 | 6.4 | 5.5 |
|   Female | 5.3 | 5.0 | 5.4 | 8.6 | 7.9 | 7.3 |
| Other | 10.2 | 8.1 | 8.2 | 13.9 | 13.1 | 13.1 |
|   Male | 10.7 | 7.4 | 7.3 | 13.7 | 12.7 | 12.4 |
|   Female | 9.4 | 9.2 | 9.3 | 14.0 | 13.6 | 14.0 |

Source: *1978 Statistical Abstract of the U.S.*

The picture becomes even bleaker when the unemployment rate for minority youth is examined. See Table 3 for these statistics.

## Table 3

### Minority Youth Unemployment

### August 1980

| | |
|---|---|
| Native American | 60.0% |
| Black | 37.4% |
| Hispanic | 19.1% |

Source: *1980 Statistical Abstract of the U.S.*

Minorities generally do not have equal access to basic health services, much less preventative health care. This results in or contributes to shorter life expectancies, more infant and maternal deaths and even, in the extreme, exacerbation of disease as minorities are used as unwitting "guinea pigs" for white scientists. Racists believe that minorities die younger and are sick more frequently because of inherent physical inferiority; in reality, the institutional racism of health care practices, facilities and personnel, combined with poverty and deprivation, produces such results.

The statistics in Table 4 on infant and maternal deaths, gathered from the United States National Center for Health Statistics, portray the problem in all its starkness.

---

## Table 4

*Infant and Maternal Death Rates* (per 1,000 live births except as noted)

|  | 1965 | 1970 | 1971 | 1972 | 1973 | 1974 | 1975 | 1976 |
|---|---|---|---|---|---|---|---|---|
| 1. Infant Deaths[1] | 24.7 | 20.0 | 19.1 | 18.5 | 17.7 | 16.7 | 16.1 | 15.2 |
| White | 21.5 | 17.8 | 17.1 | 16.4 | 15.8 | 14.8 | 14.2 | 13.3 |
| Other | 40.3 | 30.9 | 28.5 | 27.7 | 26.2 | 24.9 | 24.2 | 23.5 |
| 2. Maternal Deaths | 31.6 | 21.5 | 18.8 | 18.8 | 15.2 | 14.6 | 12.8 | 12.3 |
| White | 21.0 | 14.4 | 13.0 | 14.3 | 10.7 | 10.0 | 9.1 | 9.0 |
| Other | 83.7 | 55.9 | 45.3 | 38.5 | 34.6 | 35.1 | 29.0 | 26.5 |
| 3. Fetal Deaths[2] | 16.2 | 14.2 | 13.4 | 12.7 | 12.2 | 11.5 | 10.7 | 10.5 |
| White | 13.9 | 12.4 | 11.8 | 11.2 | 10.8 | 10.2 | 9.5 | 9.3 |
| Other | 27.2 | 22.6 | 21.2 | 19.5 | 18.6 | 17.0 | 16.0 | 15.2 |
| 4. Neonatal Deaths[3] | 17.7 | 15.1 | 14.2 | 13.6 | 13.0 | 12.3 | 11.6 | 10.9 |
| White | 16.1 | 13.8 | 13.0 | 12.4 | 11.8 | 11.1 | 10.4 | 9.7 |
| Other | 25.4 | 21.4 | 19.6 | 19.2 | 17.2 | 17.2 | 16.8 | 16.3 |

---

[1]Deaths of infants less than 1 year old, exclusive of neonatal deaths.
[2]Stillbirths.
[3]Deaths of infants less than 28 days old, exclusive of fetal deaths.

To translate these impersonal numbers into something more identifiable, let's look at this example. It is 1976 and you are a pregnant Hispanic woman. A white friend of yours is also pregnant and due to have her baby around the same time you are expecting yours. Her chances of having a miscarriage are almost 1 in 100. Your chances of miscarrying are 50 percent higher than that. Her chances of dying in childbirth or from the complications of childbirth are less than .9 percent. Yours are two and one-half times higher than hers. The chances that her baby will die in its first month of life are 1 in 100. Again, your baby's chances of dying are 50 percent higher. And her baby stands an 87 percent chance of living to see its first birthday, while your baby's chances are only 76 percent.

If your baby is a boy, his average life expectancy will be 64.1 years; your daughter's average life span will be 72.6 years. But your friend's son can expect to live an average of 69.7 years (5.6 years longer than your son) and her daughter can expect a life span average of 77.3 years (4.7 years longer than your daughter).

Further statistics provide further evidence of unequal access to good health. Migrant farm workers have 2 to 5 times the rate of respiratory and digestive diseases, 17 times as much tuberculosis and 35 times the rate of intestinal worms as does the general population. The worst health care in the United States, however, is found on Indian reservations, where residents suffer 60 times more dysentery, 30 times more strep throat, 11 times more hepatitis and 10 times more tuberculosis than do other Americans. In addition, teenage male Native Americans have the highest suicide rate of any group in the world—over 100 suicides per 100,000 per year—even though the suicide rate for Native Americans before the invasion of white men from Europe was near zero! And alcoholism causes 6½ times as many deaths among Native Americans as among the general population.

Racism at its most vile is evidenced by the fact that for 40 years the United States Public Health Service conducted a syphilis study in which 400 black men were used as medical guinea pigs. These men were left untreated, even after the penicillin cure was discovered, so that doctors could study the course of untreated syphilis. The men were never told that they had the disease.

A major civil rights issue has emerged from the closing of hospitals in inner-city areas as a direct result of budgetary restrictions. Despite arguments to the contrary, independent studies have indicated that there is a strong association between the percentage of minority population in a certain area and the likelihood that a given hospital will close. Even the Justice Department has filed one suit against a city and plans more suits because of the discriminatory impact such closings usually have.

## Racism and Education

The education system in the United States has, in the twentieth century, been the most important institution in society. Yet education has always been bound closely to racism in this country. During slavery, it was unlawful to teach slaves to read. In the North, "separate but equal" became a fact if not the rule, and by the time argument led to integration, racial cleavages had already become firmly entrenched.

Educational institutions are racist in three principal ways:
1. by giving inferior education to minority children;
2. by willfully not educating minority children in order to perpetuate existing racial inequities;
3. by miseducating white children about their own racist heritage, and minority children about their own racial history.[11]

Poor inner-city (vs suburban) schools, teachers with racist expectations for minority children's achievement (self-fulfilling prophecy), false and erroneous texts and materials (how does the Native American child feel when reading that Columbus "discovered" America?), and the tendency of administrators and guidance counselors to "track" minority students into technical-vocational or business-clerical courses of study, are but a few of the racist characteristics of the United States educational system. Perhaps the worst of these in the long run, in terms of human dignity, is the miseducation of all children: the glorification of Western Anglo-American history and culture and the denigration of African, Asian, and Native American history and culture.

Minority teacher/minority student ratios provide a glaring example of one way racism is perpetuated in the educational structure. For example, while 25 percent of the elementary and secondary school students in Denver are Hispanic, only 2.3 percent of the teachers of those children are Hispanic. Similarly, of 199 Bureau of Indian Affairs schools, only 13 are operated by the Native American communities they serve. In New York City, the ratios are as follows:

22

| Black teachers to black students | 1:84 |
| Hispanic principals to Hispanic students | 1:262 |
| White teachers to white students | 1:8 |

*Racism and Criminal Justice*

The United States Pledge of Allegiance promotes "justice for all" but that, too, is still nothing more than an ideal. From law enforcement officers to bail systems to prison populations, the deck is stacked against minorities.

For example, the statistics in Table 5 reveal a massive imbalance between the numbers of white and black officers on city police forces. That is, in major American cities where minorities constitute over 40 percent of the population, they contribute only 5 percent of the police officers. In other words, if you are a minority person, your chance of dealing with a white, not a minority, police officer is overwhelming, and consequently, so is your chance of encountering discriminatory treatment by the law. Such inequality led to, among other things, the organization of the Black Panther Party and the Deacons for Defense and Justice.

---

## Table 5

### Percent of White Population and White Police Officers of Some Major American Cities

| City | % White Population | % White Police |
|------|-------------------|----------------|
| Atlanta | 52 | 90 |
| Baltimore | 49 | 93 |
| Boston | 79 | 98 |
| Buffalo | 72 | 97 |
| Dayton | 64 | 96 |
| Detroit | 51 | 95 |
| Memphis | 52 | 95 |
| New Orleans | 49 | 96 |
| Oakland | 59 | 96 |
| St. Louis | 53 | 89 |
| District of Columbia | 27 | 79 |

(Source: Report of the National Advisory Commission on Civil Disorders, 1968, p. 321.)

The bail system provides another example of the glaring inequality in the criminal justice system in the United States. The judge can, in most cases, set bail at any amount he chooses, usually relative to the alleged crime and the defendant's financial circumstances. However, more often than not, statistics show that minority-urban bail is consistently higher than white-suburban bail. In addition, poor people who cannot post bail are convicted more often and sentenced more harshly than those released pending trial.

Average sentences in federal prisons (Table 6) also show some interesting trends:

## Table 6

|  | Whites | Minorities |
|---|---|---|
| Average Sentence | 42.9 months | 57.5 months |
| Income Tax Evasion (average) | 12.8 months | 28.6 months |
| Drug Abuse (average) | 61.1 months | 81.1 months |

In addition, while 12 percent of the population of the United States, according to the 1970 census, is black, 42 percent of the nation's prisoners are black. Further, white prisoners enjoy more acquittals and more suspended sentences. Of all prisoners executed since 1930, 53.5 percent have been black. Over half of the convicted rapists were white, but of the 455 men executed for rape, only 48 were white.

An exacerbation of the whole issue occurs when, as in New York State (scene of the Attica Prison massacre), over 90 percent of the corrections officials are white, while 60 percent of the prison population is non-white.

## Racism and the Mass Media

Mass media—newspapers, magazines, television and radio—have become pervasive and influential shapers of attitudes. Yet, until very recently, the only faces seen on television were white, and the news reported in print was written, published and edited by whites for whites. The mass media are still predominantly white-owned. Take a look at the following statistics.

24

- Of 1,772 daily and 7,553 weekly newspapers in the United States, 216 are minority-owned (4 daily and 212 weekly), or 2 percent.
- Of 6,500 American publishing houses, 25 are minority-owned, or .03 percent.
- Of 730 commercial television stations, 3 are minority-owned, or .04 percent.
- Of 8,000 radio stations, 30 are minority-owned, or .03 percent.

On the staffs of the white-owned stations and papers, minorities hold a disproportionately lower number of jobs. In an industry that reaches virtually every person in the United States (96 percent of the population own at least one television set), this underrepresentation has serious implications for the ways in which minorities see themselves in a larger context, the ways whites see minorities (if they see them at all), and the ways whites see themselves.

Some recent changes have been purely cosmetic—putting at least one non-white into most television commercials, for example—and some changes have even perpetuated racism—stereotyping minorities in the ubiquitous "situation comedies."

On the other hand, the success of mini-series such as *Roots* and the slowly increasing additional programming showing minority persons behaving realistically in realistic situations are beginning to have an effect. However, until minorities find themselves in positions that include the power to select and direct programming in a comprehensive way, the going will be slow.

## Ethnic Response to Oppression

The story of ethnic minorities in North America is something more than the record of white aggression, racism, discrimination, lynchings, broken agreements, intermittent remorse, prolonged failure, nativist bigotry and repressive acts. It is also a record of the minorities' survival, adaptation, creativity, faith, hope and protest, both covert and overt, in the face of overwhelming obstacles.

Religion, and specifically the Christian church, has played an important role in the minority response to oppression. While the necessity for ethnic churches and their continued existence are a judgment on Christianity and an indictment of the American Christian churches, for most ethnic groups the ethnic church has provided a place of gathering and an environment where they could enjoy fellowship, create their own institutions, preserve their culture, and not have to apologize for being who they are. In some sense this was an external acculturation process to adopt "Westernized ways," but in a more important sense it was an adaptive response to ethnic oppression and an active, creative retreat from the daily tensions of repressing one's own culture and attempting to be accepted by the white majority.

Here we discover the creative genius of ethnic minority theological reflection and the beauty of religion created on these shores out of the many converging influences. Religion becomes the organizing principle of these ethnic minorities and the visible center of life. The ethnic churches become caring institutions, both out of necessity and in obedience to their Lord. At the same time their very existence and their application of the meaning of the gospel protested the majority ideology.

Out of this creativity, each ethnic group now brings its gifts, and the truth it has discovered, to be boldly placed on the altars of the church. Such a pluralistic sharing may yet enable God's people to be more faithful to the meaning of the gospel and to the judgment and grace of God in a society bedevilled by the demons of hedonism, classism, racism and sexism, and in a church obsessed with pop religion and biblicism that threaten to transform the revolutionary ethic of Jesus into an inoffensive prudential morality. In our living, and in our thinking, we must tap these subterranean streams which flow together at the deepest levels of our common humanity and needs.

It is to this task that the church must turn its attention and use all of the resources available to it. "For we are strangers before thee, and sojourners, as all our fathers were; our days on the earth are like a shadow, and there is no abiding. . . . Thine, O Lord, is the greatness, and the power, and the glory, and the victory, and the majesty; for all that is in the heavens and in the earth is thine; thine is the kingdom, O Lord, and thou art exalted as head above all" (I Chronicles 29:15, 11).

# CHAPTER 1: RECALL/RESPONSE

## RECALL

"Out of [its] creativity, each ethnic group now brings its gifts, and the truth it has discovered, to be boldly placed on the altars of the church. . . . In our living, and in our thinking, we must tap these subterranean streams [the many ethnic and racial cultures] which flow together at the deepest levels of our common humanity and needs."

## RESPONSE

(1) Each of us has roots—cultural, ethnic, racial. That is a part of our journey as persons. And we cannot understand others until we have understood ourselves. In small groups: Write a short racial and/or ethnic history of your family and their pilgrimage to the United States or Canada, e.g., from where did they come? When? Why? etc.

(2) Can you cite a negative incident you or one of your ancestors experienced in North America or elsewhere because of your ethnic and/or racial origin? How did it feel?

(3) Can you recall your first encounter with a member of an ethnic or racial group different from your own? What happened? How did you feel?

(4) Bring to mind your most recent encounter with a person from another ethnic or racial group. What, if anything, is different in this encounter from your first?

(5) Do you feel that you are oppressed because of your racial and/or ethnic identity? In what way? How do you handle your feelings?

(6) In your daily life what points of contact do you have with persons of racial groups different from your own?

    (a) live in my neighborhood

    (b) work with me

    (c) attend same church

    (d) meet socially

    (e) attend school with me or my children

    (f) members of my extended family

    (g) other (specify)

    (h) none of the above

Would you like to change the points of contact? How? Why?

# 2

# RACE, PREJUDICE AND RACISM

Scientists have reached general agreement in recognizing that all people are one, i.e., that all belong to the same species, *homo sapiens*. The term "race" is generally used to refer to the major divisions within the species. In the eighteenth century, beginning with Linnaeus (1738), the human race was divided into three primary groups: Mongoloids (Asians, Eskimos), Negroids and Caucasians.[1]

## The Three Primary Racial Groups

These three groups differ from one another in a series of racial *traits*, which are genetically determined. Certain traits easily recognizable and well established as hereditary include: head shape, facial form, nasal form, skin color, hair color, hair texture, eye color, etc. These traits, or sorting criteria, have been formed and informed to a small extent by such elements as natural selection, environmental factors and hybridization. The high correlation between form and function has been obvious for centuries. For example, the Mongoloid race, especially its northern half (e.g., Eskimos) is a typical cold-area race. The Mongoloids were short of stature, stocky, through conservation of body fat for food and warmth, with thick skin, small flat noses that do not freeze easily and narrow eyeslits that protect against driving snow and desert sand. On the other hand, Negroids tended to be long-legged, for speed, and dark-skinned, for protection from the tropical sun. The Caucasians generally did not have such striking physical characteristics. Evolving mainly in temperate zones, they are characterized by general intermediate adaptation, and their physical traits are more diluted and exhibit a wider degree of variance, including both the very fair, blue-eyed, blond Nords and olive-skinned, brown-eyed and dark-haired Mediterranean peoples.

A race—from a biological and anthropological standpoint—can be defined as one of the populations constituting the species *homo sapiens*. Often geographical barriers kept these populations more or less separated, limiting interbreeding. Migration, however, has increased dramatically within the last two centuries, and the distinguishing racial traits so clear to early anthropologists are becoming less clear as the world's gene pool becomes more intermixed. The biological processes which inform the anthropological classification of "races" are thus not static at all, it is important to note, but dynamic—they were not the same 200 years ago as they are now, and we have every reason to expect that they will continue to change.

In short, the term "race" relates to the frequency and distribution of hereditary genes or physical characteristics which appear, fluctuate and often disappear in the course of time by reason of geographic and/or cultural isolation. Those physical differences essentially distinguish one race from another.

## The Ethnic Group

Closely akin to this concept of "race," but fundamentally different from it, is the concept of "a people," or "an ethnic group." Such a group is a sociological entity, the product of an historical and cultural process. It is united by one or more of many factors, including a common history, origin, or tribe; nationality; language; religion; value system; or geography. Such ethnic groups are not static or fixed, but can become larger or smaller and more or less exclusive.

Ethnic group identity is generally acquired at birth. Babies acquire a *name*, an individual name, a family name and a group name, and they acquire the heritage, the origins and *history*, of the group into which they are born. The group's cultural past automatically endows the offspring with *nationality*, or regional or tribal affiliation, *language, religion* and a *value system*—all of which have immediate impact on the shaping of the babies' outlook and way of life from the first moment of existence.

This legacy of the past is a part of these children's lives almost before they come to any consciousness at all. They also come into possession of a whole series of present circumstances: the family's relative wealth or poverty, its relative position in the larger groups to which it belongs, the group's position in relation to other groups in the environment—the relatedness of the individual and the group to the world.

The basic ethnic group identity is a most crucial ingredient in the individual's sense of belonging. Obviously, this need *can be* and often *is* satisfied to differing degrees in person-to-person contexts, or in one or more o. the many other secondary group identities acquired in the course of a lifetime in all the different collectivities to which an individual belongs—class, social, educational, occupational, professional and recreational. But these secondary sources of belonging-ness serve effectively only when basic group identity does not get in the way, and they are more likely to function effectively when the secondary groups are homogeneous, where the basic identity is shared by all.

An individual *belongs* to a group, in the deepest sense, with the realization that he/she is not alone and that, remaining in and of a group, he/she cannot be rejected or denied. The identity can be abandoned but cannot be taken away.

Group identification, as it relates to minority groups of all kinds, is promoted in several different ways: organizations, newspapers and magazines targeted toward that group alone; institutions developed apart from the general "American" community life, especially churches and the schools, social clubs, youth groups and recreational associations that they spawn. The use of a "foreign" tongue—be it a language different from English or just a different usage of English—is a very conscious and effective means of forging a cohesive group that excludes those who are not a part of it.

When persons come together in groups, a new influence begins to operate that cannot be explained through analysis of the separate personalities of the group's members. That is not to say that the individuals take on a homogeneous group personality, but merely that the whole is greater than the sum of its parts. Chemistry provides a useful analogy: an analysis of the individual properties of hydrogen and oxygen would not begin to explain the properties of water, which results from their *interaction*.

## The Misuse of "Race" and "Ethnicity"

Unfortunately, most people confuse the concept of "race" with the concept of "ethnic group." They use "race" to refer to any group of people distinguishable by nationality, religion, language, geography or culture. Within the true meaning of the term, however,

Canadians, for example, are not a race, nor are citizens of the United States, nor any of the major national groups. Catholics and Jews are not a race, nor are any religious groups. People who speak Japanese, or English, do not comprise a race. The people who live in India, or Ireland, are not a race, nor are people who are culturally Arab or Pakistani.

National, religious, linguistic, geographic and cultural groups do not necessarily coincide with racial groups: the traits of such groups have no genetic connection with racial traits. Instead, these traits of "shared sameness" are the common holdings of a sub-group, the *social* features.

Whatever classification anthropologists decide upon, mental, cultural and/or moral characteristics are *never* part of racial classification.

Folk beliefs concerning innate racial and national temperaments have persisted for centuries and provide the basis for widely held and long-lived stereotypes. Interestingly, "tests" for such factors have been unsuccessful in obtaining representative samples, and in controlling such factors as education, motivation, rapport, socioeconomic background and language.

The notion of biologically superior or biologically inferior races is equally fallacious. For example, government statistics readily evidence significant differences in disease, infant mortality and life expectancy rates in the United States between whites and non-whites. What the numbers do not and cannot show are differences in health education, housing, nutrition and medical care—especially early diagnosis and adequate treatment.

Perhaps the most insidious, damaging and widespread belief is the notion of mentally superior or mentally inferior races. The belief that some groups have greater innate intellectual capacity goes back at least as far as Aristotle, who justified slavery on the grounds that nature intended some men to rule and others to serve. Early sociologists reinforced this belief with their contention that the primitive (i.e., pre-literate or pre-"civilized") mind was incapable of logic— unable to separate ideas or objects from the emotions and sentiments engendered by them. This issue is alive and well even today. Some prominent educators and social scientists, such as Arthur Jensen and Donald Shockley, say that yes, fundamental and intrinsic problems in education, health and society in general are reflected in group differences in testing and intelligence (i.e., blacks score lower on I.Q. tests than whites because of discriminatory practices which have affected them as a group) *but* continue to maintain that, collectively, black persons are "intellectually inferior" by reason of heredity as well. Jensen goes so far as to quantify the difference: "between one-half and three-fourths of the average I.Q. difference between American Negroes and whites is attributable to genetic factors, and the remainder to environmental factors and their interaction with the genetic differences."[2] In arriving at this conclusion, Jensen dismisses such contributing factors as differences in socioeconomic status (he considers the criticism too nonspecific); negative correlations between environment and ability (he says that groups such as American Indians are *more* disadvantaged than Negroes); culture-biased tests (he points to data indicating that translating the Stanford-Binet into Negro ghetto dialect does not improve scores); language deprivation (he says children born deaf are the most verbally deprived group available for study, yet they perform better than Negroes on the nonverbal parts of intelligence tests); nutritional deficiencies (he argues that children in India with much poorer nutritional and health care than American Negroes score higher at age 6 on nonverbal ability tests).

When such a thesis gets widespread visibility—and such theses do, because they lend scientific credibility to racist belief-systems—there is always great danger that theory will become *self-fulfilling prophecy*, discouraging the accomplishments and aspirations of the group labelled "inferior" and limiting the expectations of all those who deal with members of that group. And as the prophecy fulfills itself, data to support the theory grow

What usually gets lost in the process of identifying races with cultural, mental or moral characteristics is the realization that race is an anthropological and biological classification that *in and of itself* is not important. As we have seen at the begining of this chapter, in fact, there are no "pure" races as such, because of the infinitesimal variations in individual genes; and the less isolated and the more mobile a particular group has been, the greater the problem in classifying it within a race. Each population of the species *homo sapiens* differs from the others in the frequency of one or more genes. Because those genes that control such factors as eye color or hair texture, and are thus responsible for the hereditary differences among peoples, are few when compared to the whole genetic make-up of a person and to the vast numbers of genes common to all human beings, it follows that the similarities among humans are far greater than the differences.

When race is used to classify people *socially*, when race is used as a *symbol* to set people apart for differential treatment, the term, with all its inaccuracies, becomes a weapon.

## The Dynamics of Prejudice and Racism

Then what accounts for the amazing persistence of prejudice and racism from one generation to another, across an international array of differences, and in the face of all the available scientific facts? To answer this question, we must look not only at the existence of racism and prejudice, but at their underlying psychological and social functions.

What we are really dealing with here is a matter of relationships, and the personal and social mechanisms by which these relationships are maintained, rather than with a simple arithmetical concept of majority-minority. As a matter of fact, there are counties in the state of Mississippi where there are three times as many black residents as white residents. In Zimbabwe and South Africa the ratio of blacks to whites is overwhelmingly higher. In colonial India, there were thousands of native Indians for every Englishman. From such facts the message becomes clear: a discussion of minority-majority situations is concerned not with numerical proportions, but with a pattern of relationships, with the distribution of power.

While Anglo-Saxons are the largest single identifiable group in the United States, according to the Census Bureau, they are only 14 percent of the population—not a much larger group than German-Americans (13 percent) or blacks (11 percent). Yet "WASP" dominance, prestige and economic and political power belie that numerical relationship, and maintain that upper hand by a variety of stratagems.

*Prejudice, Racism and the Individual*

It was Gordon Allport, the great Harvard psychologist, who first understood and explored the dynamics of prejudice and racism in the

34

individual. Such attitudes, he pointed out in *The ABC's of Scapegoating*,[3] actually serve to meet deep emotional needs within the personality of the individual who holds them.

When an individual member of a sub-group of the dominant faction in a society experiences failure, or even stress, the experience activates a need to lash out against someone, to seek someone onto whom the blame can be affixed, onto whom one's aggressive tendencies and failures can be projected—in short, a scapegoat.

Minorities have often been used as a scapegoat by the dominant group in a society. The ideal scapegoat group meets several or all of the following list of criteria, and racial minority groups usually do: (1) The minority must be highly visible, outstanding in anything from skin color to shape of nose or religious customs. (2) The minority cannot be too strong or have the power necessary to retaliate. (3) The minority must be readily accessible—ghettos of all types are very useful here in that they effectively isolate the minority and make them easy targets. (4) The minority may have previously been an object of blame, thereby allowing the majority access to latent hostility. (5) The minority should personify some idea that is disliked by the dominant group.

Allport's frustration-aggression theory of racial prejudice thus contends that prejudice provides a socially approved channel of expressing aggression after the experience of frustration and failure, even when that frustration and failure have nothing whatsoever to do with the minority in question.

From a slightly different psychological approach, prejudice may be seen as a refuge for the inadequate personality.

> Prejudice is our method of transferring our own sickness to others. It is our ruse for disliking others rather than ourselves. We find absolution in our prejudices. We find also in them an enemy made to order rather than inimical forces out of our control. . . . Prejudice is a raft onto which the shipwrecked mind clambers and paddles to safety.[4]

This is not necessarily to say that prejudice is pathology, that prejudiced individuals are either neurotic or psychotic, but that racial prejudice is a function of personality, and not simply an isolated and independent attitude. As Allport puts it, "Prejudice is more than an incident in many lives; it is often lock-stitched into the very fabric of personality."[5] He finds that the following characteristics are "earmarks of a personality in whom prejudice is functionally important":[6]

(1) Ambivalence toward parents: A relationship of power, rather than love, prevails.

(2) Moralism: Rigidity with respect to moralism—not a true moralism but one which is tense, compulsive and projective.

(3) Dichotomization: Things are black or white with no varying shades of gray. People are good or bad; there is a right way and a wrong way, weak and strong, pure and impure.

(4) Need for definiteness: Intolerance toward ambiguity. The person always has an opinion and demands a clear-cut structure of the world.

(5) Externalization: The prejudiced person believes that things happen *to* him, they are not caused *by* him. He feels little control over his destiny.

(6) Institutionalization: Devotion to institutions, whether patriotic, religious or social, which seems to satisfy the need and hunger for safety and security.

(7) Authoritarianism: No great fondness for individualism, freedom, democracy, social change. Instead, this person prefers authority, definite power arrangements, discipline, strong leaders and an orderly society.

The personality tendencies noted above—rigidity of mind, for example—that have been positively correlated with prejudice do not necessarily *cause* that prejudice. Indeed, it may be the other way around. There are those who maintain that racial and ethnic prejudice are part of our cultural pattern; normal, accepted and well-adjusted individuals conform to and abide by the standards and conventions of their society, which include the norms of prejudice and discrimination. To this way of thinking the rebellious individuals, the nonconformists—and the tolerant and nonprejudiced—are the ones who are deviant.

## Institutional and Cultural Racism

Racism and prejudice exist in dimensions beyond the dual personality. They have institutional and cultural dimensions, as well. Stokely Carmichael has described it aptly:

> When white terrorists bomb a black church and kill five black children, that is an act of individual racism . . . but when in the same city five hundred black babies die each year because of lack of proper food, shelter and medical facilities, and thousands more are destroyed and maimed physically, emotionally and intellectually because of conditions of poverty and discrimination in the black community, that is a function of institutional racism.[7]

In this institutional dimension, prejudice serves another very important function: it facilitates the exploitation of minorities in order to increase the prestige, power and economic gains of the majority. Tolerance has turned to intolerance when a minority group has begun to encroach on the business of others. The Chinese in California, for example, were held in esteem as long as they confined themselves to enterprises whites had no interest in, such as hand laundries. Violent antipathy arose, however, when they sought to expand into other, more "desirable" occupations, but subsided when they withdrew into their Chinatowns and their "acceptable" vocations.

In North American society as a whole, the intensity and nature of feeling toward immigrants has been closely related to economic conditions. Prejudice is stimulated during periods of depression/recession and general economic unrest.

With the passage of time, dominant-to-minority relationships in the United States have gradually sorted out into a hierarchy of oppression-exclusion. Eventually, we find ourselves dealing with a light-dark spectrum in which those with the lightest skins are generally at the "top," or most advantageous, end of the scale, while those with the darkest skins are at the "bottom," or most oppressed end of the scale.

One brief—and imperfect—example of this color spectrum can be seen in Table 7. Based on the 1970 United States census, it lists several American ethnic groups and their average family incomes in relation to the national average for a family.

## Table 7

| Ethnicity | Income |
|---|---|
| Jewish | 170% |
| Japanese | 132% |
| Polish | 115% |
| Italian | 112% |
| German | 107% |
| Anglo-Saxon | 107% |
| Irish | 103% |
| NATIONAL AVERAGE | 100% |
| Chinese | 99% |
| Filipino | 99% |
| West Indian | 94% |
| Mexican | 76% |
| Puerto Rican | 63% |
| Black | 62% |
| Indian (Native American) | 60% |

Source: *Essays and Data on American Ethnic Groups*,
        Urban Institute, 1978

While one minority group of color—the Japanese—had average incomes higher than the national average, *all* of the groups below the national average line are minority groups of color, and the lowest of these are also the darkest. It is also noteworthy that *no* white groups fell below the national average. This is an instance of the color spectrum at work in minority-majority relationships.

## Danger: Prejudice and Racism at Work

The institutional use of prejudice to increase the prestige, income and power of the dominant group becomes a fixed part of a culture. Prejudice is embodied in the lore of the society, developed in its literature and built into its institutions. Prejudice carries with it a whole series of convictions about the inferiority of minority culture, and at this point, when the prejudice combines with the power to sustain such convictions, the result is racism. Reduced to its simplest elements: Prejudice plus Power equals Racism.

This is the furnace in which individual and institutional racism are forged into a single instrument of exclusion and oppression. In *Prejudice and Racism*,[8] Jones diagrams the telescoping problems of individual and institutional racism as shown in Figure 1:

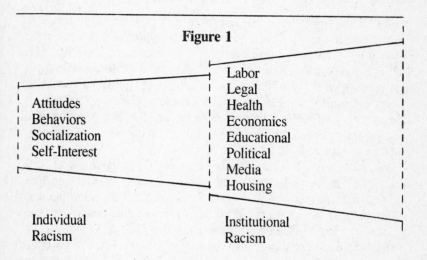

**Figure 1**

Attitudes
Behaviors
Socialization
Self-Interest

Labor
Legal
Health
Economics
Educational
Political
Media
Housing

Individual
Racism

Institutional
Racism

Not many of us are able to free ourselves from the racism and prejudice which are the warp and woof of our daily living. As the National Education Association's publication, *Education and Racism,* put it in 1973:

All white individuals in our society are racist. Even if a white is totally free from all conscious racial prejudices, he [sic] remains a racist, for he receives benefits distributed by a white racist society through its institutions. Our institutional and cultural processes are so arranged as to automatically benefit whites, just because they are white.

It is essential for whites to recognize that they receive most of these racist benefits automatically, unconsciously and unintentionally.

Racism can take various shapes and forms. It can be overt and clearly manifested, as in the recent resurgence of the Ku Klux Klan, yet often it takes more subtle forms.

More common, no less real is the racism of persons who harbor discriminatory attitudes yet consider themselves blameless as long as they observe the letter of the law.[9]

Individuals who are racist are often in a position of power over minority persons—and often have great opportunity to put their racism into practice. Some everyday examples are the teacher who threatens to punish Hispanic or Native American children for using a language other than English in the classroom, the guidance counselor who puts minority children into "lower track" classes without evaluating their past performance or aptitudes, and the shop foreman who assigns menial tasks to minorities while allowing whites the opportunity to learn new skills and advance.

Racism on an individual level has become so pervasive and unconscious that even well-intentioned individuals may be unaware that they are manifesting it in their behavior or speech. For example, how often do we use the adjective "black" to connote the negative or the pejorative? How often do we hear the terms "black Monday," or "black magic," or "blacken his reputation" used? How often are the words "whiter than snow, Lord, wash me just now" sung in white Protestant churches? Why are liberation fighters in South Africa referred to by the media as "terrorists" or "guerillas" while Europeans who opposed Nazism during World War II were referred to as members of the "Resistance"? During the 60's, blacks who demonstrated were called rioters, while white university students were called demonstrators.[10] It is individual racism that spurs adult Sunday school participants, "upstanding" Christians and dedicated church workers all, to state, "Yes, I think minorities should have good housing, but I don't want them living next door to *me* on Maple Street," or, "Blacks are responsible for their own bad housing. If they'd take care of it and not tear it apart, they'd be okay."

These are just a few examples of the ways in which members of the dominant white group maintain their position of dominance, hold onto their power and prestige, and preserve their way of life. A docile, subservient but separate and distant minority can be very useful, but such a minority becomes a menace when it grows restless, seeks to change its status and aspires to new roles. Dominant groups then must devise techniques, agencies and policies of control. When the "problem" appears to be more than individuals can handle, the "solution" gets built into the majority's policies, procedures, habits and acts—institutional racism occurs.

Institutional racism is a two-edged sword: it serves not only to subjugate and subordinate the minority, but to accrue gains—social, economic and otherwise—to the majority. "Redlining" is a good example of such institutional racism. Minority families are prevented from purchasing homes in certain "off-limits" areas in two ways: banks in those areas refuse to make mortgage loans to them and real estate agents refuse to sell to them even if they have mortgage money from somewhere else. Institutions support both of these patterns of racism, and both institutional patterns are extensions of individual racism.

Some patterns of institutional racism are not direct extensions of conscious racist decisions or acts, but occur when the norms of an institution are predicated on assumptions of equality of treatment that are not met in the actual practices of society. The application of the institution's "equitable" policies and procedures then produces racist results. For example, the person charged with a crime has a legal right to trial by a jury of peers. But seldom do minority persons get such trials. The judicial system of the United States is based on an assumption of cultural and racial homogeneity that does not exist.

Thus a retarded black man in Alabama can be convicted of rape by a jury of twelve white men and women, and four white policemen in Florida can be acquitted of charges of murdering a black man by a jury of six white men. The American judicial system has many glaring inequalities, and racism is one of the most obvious.

Another example of institutional racism is the use of standardized test scores as criteria for employment and for admission to colleges and to graduate and law schools. Not only are such tests generally culturally biased against minorities, but the effects of racism in economics, real estate and primary and secondary education often make these tests unrepresentative and poor predictors of "success" for minorities. To use test scores alone as the basis for exclusion from (or admission to) white institutions is thus a racist practice. As civil rights activist Dick Gregory puts it:

Basically black folks in America do not hate white folks. We hate this stinking white racist system with these stinking white racist institutions, not you. The United States Constitution that gives a man freedom of expression gives you a right to hate me. Individual racism we're not worried about. It's this damn institutionalized racism that's choking us to death. Here's what black folks is talking about today: a white racist system that keeps me locked in a black ghetto all my life so I've got to develop a different culture to survive with the rats and the roaches. And when I break out and come to your institutions, you ask me the wrong tests. You don't ask me about the ghetto. You ask me about the Eiffel Tower.[11]

Only in recent years have such practices been understood as racist. A thumbnail definition of institutional racism would be: those established laws, customs and practices which systematically reflect and produce racial inequities in society. If racist consequences result from such laws, customs and practices, then the institution is racist, whether or not the individuals maintaining those practices are racist themselves or have racist intentions.

Again, institutional racism can be intentional or unintentional. While intentionality is usually quite clear, unintentional racism can be very ambiguous. For example, when in the early 70's the state of Massachusetts enacted a law which demanded that school systems be racially balanced or lose state financial support, it also prohibited the building of new schools that were to be attended by a substantial majority of one race. The purpose of the law was to promote racial integration in the public schools and thereby to provide better educational opportunities for minority children. However, one of the consequences was that city administrators used the law to suspend the building of new schools in minority neighborhoods and communities. Thus already overcrowded classrooms in those neighborhoods and communities became even more crowded and educational opportunities became even fewer. Whether the administrators used the law or allowed the law to use them—whatever the intentionality—racist practices were allowed to continue and were even exacerbated.[12]

Institutions have great *power* to reward or penalize. They reward by providing opportunities and penalize by withholding them. They reward by providing career opportunities for some people and foreclosing them for others. They reward as well by the way social benefits are distributed—by deciding who receives training and skills, medical care, formal education, political influence, moral support and self-respect, productive employment, fair treatment by the law, decent housing, self-confidence and promise of a secure future for self and children.[13]

Some institutions are indeed attempting to change their racist patterns. Many of the Protestant denominations in the United States have established task forces charged with eliminating institutional racism at all levels of church life. When the Catholic bishops of the United States met in November of 1979, they voted on a proposed national pastoral letter on racism as a part of a five-year plan of action for justice aimed at overcoming all forms of racism in both church and society. Similar committees are at work within the church life of Canada. And under the impetus of a $14 million class action suit, even such a company as American Telephone and Telegraph has been dissuaded from its racist and sexist practices.

In any case, some institutions are trying to make corrections, whatever their motivations. Not until such changes reach the top echelons of power and influence in this country, however, can we expect any real "progress" to be made.

43

## A Call to a Pluralistic Approach

Prejudice and racism, both individual and institutional, are pervasive in this country. While the problems as they relate to certain institutions—economics, education, criminal justice, the media—have been touched upon here, institutional racism exists in virtually every institution in this society, whether by intention or ignorance, design or effect.

Intentional institutional racism can be attributed to the institutionalization of individual racist attitudes and desires. Unintentional racist consequences can arise from either the functioning of institutions to favor the dominant group (as opposed to disfavoring minorities) or fallacious cultural assumptions upon which institutions are based and which effectively close out minority persons. In either case, we must work to eradicate prejudice and racism in all spheres of faith and life if we are to play any meaningful role in the days ahead.

Global living requires global citizens. We must become partners with others to make our world a place where every person is accepted, appreciated and respected as a member of the human family, a place where no person is kept a stranger at home.

## CHAPTER 2: RECALL/RESPONSE

## RECALL

"Then what accounts for the amazing persistence of prejudice and racism from one generation to another, across an international array of differences, and in the face of all the available scientific facts? . . . What we are really dealing with here is a matter of relationships, and the personal and social mechanisms by which these relationships are maintained . . . ."

# RESPONSE

(1) Identify each of the following groups with its appropriate term:

                                  *Race*        *Nationality*       *Religion*

A. Anglo-Saxon
B. Jew
C. Eskimo
D. White
E. Chinese
F. Black
G. Slavic
H. Canadian
I. Muslim
J. Ethiopian
K. Hispanic
L. Lebanese
M. Native American

Clarify as a group any disagreements that develop.

(2) A white woman named Lena took her black fiance to meet her family. Her father announced that he would never accept the marriage. He indicated that he considered his future son-in-law to be genetically inferior, and told him to his face that their children would be defective. In an effort to prevent the marriage, attempts were made to persuade Lena's pastor to refuse to perform the ceremony. The pastor would not listen. But members of the parents' church did write anonymous hate letters to the couple, one of which was signed ''The Voice of Your Conscience.'' Similar situations arise often. If you found yourself a member of this church, what would you do, if anything, to raise the questions of Christian responsibility in the local church? If called on by your pastor for assistance in preparing a sermon to address the issue, what specific suggestions would you offer? What would be your response to a neighbor who confided that she was the writer of one of the letters?

(3) Definitions of racism have abounded. Anthropologists, sociologists, the Kerner Commission, ministers, civil rights leaders and others have given numerous ones. They seem to be far away from the personal reality of racism. Beginning with the following words, construct your own ''definitions'' of racism using the following as an example:

45

*Native American is . . . learning in school that Columbus "disco-vered" America.*

    a) Black is . . .
    b) Native American is . . .
    c) Asian is . . .
    d) Institutional racism is . . .
    e) Hispanic is . . .

(4) Cite instances of institutional and individual racism—both overt and covert—you have experienced or witnessed in your community, school, church, etc.

(5) A recent study of cancer by the American Cancer Society shows that survival rates among cancer victims are 41 percent for whites as opposed to only 30 percent for minorities. Statistically, however, the study showed that both whites and minorities suffer from the disease in proportion to their population; i.e., minorities and whites have an equal chance of getting the disease. What factors would account for the disparity in the survival rates? How do these illustrate institutional racism?

(6) The committee on mission in a local church proposes a study on poverty and racism for the fall quarter. The proposal meets considerable opposition. An influential member of the church summarizes the feelings of the opposition: "Why do we still have to study racism? We have made tremendous progress in this area. Minority groups no longer experience prejudice and discrimination. Housing is open. Nobody prevents them from voting. Several blacks are serving in the highest chambers of government. Anybody who works hard and tries can achieve whatever they will in this society. It is time we now moved on to some other areas of our life that are more pressing and relevant, like environmental problems, economics and how we can deepen our Christian life.'" As chairperson of the committee, what response can you give? What specific facts about racism can you offer?

# 3

# CULTURE IN CRISIS

Slowly we are coming to the understanding that prejudice and racism exact from us a double price. Both the dominant and the oppressed are locked together in a relationship of mutual impoverishment. Both are separated and isolated from those with whom they ought to live in fellowship. Their understandings of their world, and of their place in the world, are diminished. The texture of daily life is made poorer.

## Culture as Life

The process by which this happens is natural enough, and understandable enough. It's just *not enough*. We are born in a specific place and at a particular time. And we experience relationships with other people, beginning usually with the family and expanding to the tribe, village, town or city, and extending to ever-broadening contacts with race, religion, nation, class or other divisions of society— all of which condition our attitudes and outlooks. The very ideas and attitudes by which we live—such concepts as time, family relationships, privacy and individuality, authority, success, physical proximity, play, work, activism, sex roles, conformity and emotional display—are shaped by the time and place in which we live. From these relationships and in these contexts we develop a sense of identity and belonging; from them, our cultural biases, values, beliefs, attitudes, behaviors, lifestyles and expectations of others are formed.

If these are not effectively challenged, however, by exposure to varied ways of life and by diverse relationships, and are not confronted by a plurality of competing views, norms or definitions of reality (what Peter Berger calls "the heretical imperative"), if they are simply supported or reinforced by those who share them, then a

47

kind of "parochial self-absorption" develops. Our own natural tendency to feel the groups to which we belong are the best, our ways the right ways, our morals superior and our religion the right and true one, takes over. Feelings of cultural superiority and a perception of our own culture as the center of the universe follow, and judgments are made on that basis. Others whose cultures may differ from ours, or persons of racial and ethnic groups different from ours, are evaluated or scaled in reference to our group.

Numerous unexamined assumptions, choices and decisions about other persons and groups—usually negative—influence and affect our relationships to the "others." Unless the whole sociocultural context can be challenged and a new understanding of the place of our own culture among other cultures emerges, individuals and structures continue to operate within a web of social norms and restraints that become oppressive and set limits on our freedom and the freedom of others. Our ability to experience and relate to those different from us as truly human persons, who share our dignity and destiny provided in God's acts of creation and redemption, is then seriously impaired.

## Cultural Arrogance in North America

The cultural phenomenon that generally happens has indeed happened in North America. For centuries, at least five distinct racial and cultural groups have been present on this continent: first, Native Americans; second, people of a mixed Spanish, Indian and African descent from Mexico, Cuba, Puerto Rico and other Latin countries; third, those of direct African descent; fourth, Asians from the Orient, including China, Japan and other Asian countries; and fifth, the Europeans. But the culture that defines life in the United States is white and European. That is, white Europeans have dominated the culture and have by and large separated themselves from the other cultural and racial groups.

This has created what Joseph Barndt has called "the cultural curtain." As he rightly points out: "the cultural style of life in the United States was determined and defined by the European descendants and was constructed primarily from the various elements of European culture."[1] All aspects of the American culture behind the curtain—lifestyles, language, art, music, values, etc.—developed to favor that which is white and Western. The culture has been

48

dominated, defined and controlled by an attitude of cultural arrogance and a myth in which white racial and cultural superiority has been maintained. Even those elements of ethnic minority cultures that have contributed to the American scene, or slipped past the curtain, have done so only with the permission of the dominant white culture, which has often consciously suppressed the cultural achievements of the minorities.

Ethnic minority cultures have been prevented from contributing to the "American culture" in a proportion sufficient to make it a truly multi-culture. Because of such cultural arrogance we have failed to deepen our own awareness of the richness in the diversity of the community of humankind which God has created and sustained through God's love of all people.

Cultural arrogance deprives the dominating group of human inter-relating with other cultures, of the beauty, values and richness to be experienced in other cultures, and of the enriched appreciation for their own deeper cultural values that can emerge from awareness of the cultures of others. Such cultural deprivation is the price cultural arrogance forces us to pay. It denies us stimulation and fosters sterility. It encourages a style of life that becomes increasingly bland and boring. It spurns the diversity and richness of human community resident in God's lavish act of creation. It forces a cultural isolation that robs us of the extravagant wealth of human cultures and drains our self-isolated culture of its own excellence, leaving us with a deterioration of values and a hedonism which cannot satisfy, an insipidness of self-expression, a discomfort with the rest of the world and an incompetence in global social relations. Yes, cultural arrogance results in cultural deprivation. More important, it leads to *cultural depravity*.

In the book of Daniel, the dramatic moment arrives, in the midst of King Bel-shazzar's extravagant feast, when the mysterious hand appears and writes upon the wall the doom of Babylon's depraved ruler. The drama may be less intense today, and cast in less personal terms. But one cannot easily avoid the feeling that our depraved culture in North America has come to a moment of challenge and of testing. The need to evaluate our position is very real.

Our cultural arrogance has left us, as a people, impoverished in spirit. Our understanding and practice of Christianity has been so deeply influenced by Western culture that often it is difficult to distinguish between the demands of the gospel for a life of obedience and the norms and values of the culture. Culturally derived concepts which are sheer relative notions have been consciously and unconsciously elevated to the stature of absolute realities.

By the nineteenth century in the United States, the goal of success and the quest for wealth and material comfort became almost inextricably tied to religion. As Ralph Gabriel puts it: "This faith and philosophy became the most persuasive siren in American life. It filled the highway with farm boys trekking to the city. It drained the towns and countryside of Europe."[2] Religion and the quest for economic success became parts of the same undertaking. Disguised as an expression of the Christian faith, the quest for material prosperity was seen as the quest to become "more joyous, more unselfish, more Christlike." We shall return later to this concept of success.

Another manifestation of the confusion between the Christian faith and the American culture is the illusion of a national character and destiny and the belief in the nation's messianic role in the world. The United States perceives the rest of the world as dependent upon it for freedom, protection, enlightenment and salvation. Because God has blessed America and chosen her for this role, the thinking goes, her every effort will be crowned with success. As Barndt has pointed out, "It is but a small step from these doctrines of superiority and infallibility to the endorsement through military action of our will on non-white and non-Western people of the world."[3]

## A Call for Self-Examination

C. Vann Woodward, an outstanding American historian, has warned against this attitude. In an analysis of the "Irony of American History," he admonishes the nation:

> We should not deceive ourselves about the opinions of other peoples. While we see ourselves as morally sound and regard our good fortune as the natural and just reward of our soundness, these views are not shared by large numbers of people in many parts of the world. They look on great wealth not as reward of our virtue but as proof of our wickedness, as evidence of the ruthless exploitation, not only of our own working people but of themselves.[4]

An international and ecumenical team of churchpersons from Africa, Asia, Latin America and Europe visiting this country in 1973 confirmed Woodward's perception. For 25 days they visited schools, social service and welfare agencies, families and churches. They explored suburbs, ghettos, minority communities, farms, rural towns, prisons and military bases. They talked with people from black, white, Hispanic, Native American and Chinese communities. They spoke with church leaders, both lay and clergy. The observations of this team of international visitors are revealing. They pointed out the close identification they had observed between American church life and American culture, and they questioned how churches could address a prophetic word to other peoples when such a close and parochial identification exists. They were amazed at the ignorance of so many Americans about foreign relations. They questioned how America could wield such enormous power in the military, economic and political spheres in the world and be so unaware of its impact on Third World nations. The team urged American churchpersons to be more sensitive to the consequences of the presence of multinational corporations in their lands and to the link between America's investment policies and support for racist and reactionary regimes. They called on American churchpersons *to reexamine their values in the light of the gospel*. Essentially, they saw that the confusion between culture and Christianity in North America is critical, and warned us of the danger of our illusions of innocence and self-righteousness.

Such reexamination of our values in the light of the gospel will require us to look at our own identity, our lifestyles, and such basic assumptions as our attitudes toward time, family relationships, privacy and individuality, authority, success, physical proximity, play, work, activism, sex roles, conformity and emotional display. To what extent do we absolutize inherited—and relative—cultural values? How does our concept of the "American Way of Life" affect our view of other cultures and people? At what points do we view the national destiny and the establishment of the kingdom of God as synonymous? At what points do we confuse the demands of the gospel with our own cultural norms? How can we act responsibly in a pluralistic society?

In an article in *Interpreter* magazine in 1973, David W. Briddell offers some guidance for the process of reexamination of our cultural values, behaviors, beliefs, cultural biases and attitudes. Briddell suggests that we cannot understand others until we have understood ourselves. Calling for church groups to engage in cross-cultural exchanges, he maintains that the effectiveness of such intercultural programs will be maximized only when "the persons involved are aware of their own assumptions, feelings and attitudes and when they attempt to understand other people's feelings and points of view rather than passing judgment upon them in terms of their own values."[5]

## The Core Attitude of American Culture

Let us take the advice of the international team discussed earlier, and shine the light of the gospel on what virtually all students of North American life agree is the central characteristic of Americans: materialism. As someone has put it, "what is not destroyed, we consume." For many years we have recklessly misused the world's goods in an effort to satisfy our seemingly insatiable appetite for material things. To be middle-class has meant, "I have the unquestioned right to buy what I want without having to justify it to anyone except the bank where I maintain my personal account." Lured and persuaded by the relentless pressure of the mass media to "grab all the gusto, you only go around once in life" and to "enjoy yourself," Americans consume 50 percent of the world's goods. They have regarded happiness, fulfillment and satisfaction as commodities that can be purchased. With credit immediately available, they have tried to satisfy all their wants. A color television set, a comfortable home, name-brand clothes, a modern automobile and frequent vacations or long weekends in Florida or the Caribbean in winter and the cool north country in summer are their minimal expectations for material comfort and convenience.

They have regarded the appalling fact that two-thirds of the world's population, mostly non-Western and non-white, are starving, as proof that these countries are *undeveloped* and thus cannot enjoy the abundant life. Meanwhile, the ghettos of major cities in this country are teeming with the poor and the powerless, the unemployed and the unemployable, but their plight is dismissed with the attitude that they are lazy and have no motivation and have not taken advantage of the opportunities that a free country offers.

Personal tastes, habits, preferences and the garnering of happiness are considered part of the private sector, where one exercises one's personal freedom. The measure of success is high consumption. The good life is material satisfaction. The proof of one's industry and ingenuity is expanded consumption.

Is this what the "pursuit of happiness" means? How can we square this social philosophy of consumerism and materialism with the demand for stewardship? How can we justify these values with the simple ethic and lifestyle of the One who said: "Foxes have holes and birds have nests, but the Son of Man has nowhere to lay his head"? If these are unquestioned ways of life, how can we expect to relate as neighbors to others whose values focus not on the quantity of material things but on the quality of human life? How do these values fit in with the search for a "just, participatory and sustainable society"? Is bigger necessarily better?

## "The Melting Pot": Success and Failure

Our cultural arrogance has thwarted and all but destroyed the ideal of "the melting pot," replacing it with the Anglo-American ideal of *assimilation*. Assimilation is the process by which groups with different cultural traits merge into a common culture. In the United States, assimilation has meant Anglo-conformity. Anglo-conformity required that those who had immigrated to America become assimilated into the host society. This means that our ethnic minorities not only take on such traits of the dominant culture as dress, language, food, consumer items and sports, but also adopt the less tangible but more important items in our discussion, such as the values, sentiments, ideas and lifestyles of the Anglo-American culture, rather than maintaining their ethnic distinctiveness.

What were these less tangible items? They were the ideal values and behaviors of the core society. The list included at least the following: the highest ideals were justice, liberty and equality; the right to own private property; individualism; and the sovereignty of the people. Other operative ideals included frugality; the nuclear family; material success as proof of moral worth; rapid personal, social, and occupational mobility; and, above all, work for its own sake. These ideals issued forth in optimism, discipline, a sense of duty, self-restraint and self-governance.

53

## The High Cost of Assimilation

Many Southern and Eastern European ethnic groups have assimilated into the white culture, often at a great price to themselves, in their sense of personal worth and identity, and to society as a whole. William Greenbaum points out, in an essay entitled "America in Search of a New Ideal: An Essay on the Rise of Pluralism," that the immigrants learned fast, asked few questions, and rose rapidly during the first decades of this century because of *shame*. They were "ashamed of their own faces, their family names, their parents and grandparents, and their class patterns, histories, and life outlooks." This shame was energized by "*hope* about becoming modern, about being secure, about escaping the wars and depressions of the old country, and about being equal with the old Americans."[6]

Spurred, lured, and led to believe that the process of assimilation would be easy, rapid, natural and inevitable, millions of Europeans crossed the Atlantic prior to World War I expecting to be melted into "the melting pot" and through a process of fusion eventually produce a great civilization and a race of "supermen." The indomitable faith of the period, and the belief that God had chosen America as a second Garden of Eden in a special act of Providence, was eloquently voiced by Israel Zangwill:

> America is God's Crucible, the great Melting Pot where all the races of Europe are melting and reforming! —Here you stand, good folk, think I, when I see you at Ellis Island, here you stand, in your fifty groups, with your fifty languages and histories, and your fifty blood hatreds and rivalries. But you won't be long like that, brothers, for these are the fires of God. A fig for your feuds and your vendettas! German and Frenchmen, Irishmen and English, Jews and Russians, into the Crucible with you all! God is making the American! . . . The real American has not yet arrived. . . . He will be the fusion of all races, perhaps the coming superman. . . . Ah, what is the glory of Rome and Jerusalem, where all races and nations come to worship and look back, compared with the glory of America, where all nations come to labour and look forward.[7]

There was an element of truth in what Zangwill expressed. The United States was indeed involved in an apprenticeship of freedom. It offered a worldwide invitation to the tired, the poor, the homeless, "the huddled masses [of Europe] yearning to breathe free." There was plenty of land and forest virgin of hunters—even the Native Americans—and plenty of coal in the bowels of the earth. There were the basic moral norms of liberty, justice and charity that are essential to any good society. There was truth in Zangwill's claim.

The error lay in the assumption that the process was easy, rapid, natural and inevitable, and that it would produce a superior people. Many books have been written by sociologists, historians and novelists about the struggles of these immigrants—the illiteracy, the quest for citizenship, the concentration in "colonies" in the cities, and more. Not enough has been written about the cultural suicide required for "successful" assimilation into an Anglo-American–dominated culture. Not enough has been said about "the North American contradiction—a universalism made up of ethnic, cultural, religious and sexual exclusions."[8] "Anglo-conformity," as Milton Gordon calls it at a later stage,[9] proved to be a heavy price to pay. The cost is still being tallied.[10]

There was a melting pot but the Protestant Americans and other Northern and Western Europeans needed not be melted in it. As Greenbaum observes: "Protestant calls for American unity were hypocritically rooted in diversity: the Protestants assumed their own exemption from the melting pot. The rest of us would become acculturated, learning their behaviors and thought patterns, but we would never be the same, never equals, much less leaders."[11] The Anglo-American conception of cultural, economic and political unity did not allow for a broad diversity of respectable lifestyles. "If we could not be the same as the Protestants, we also could not be different and be respected for our differences."[12]

## The Larger Price of Failure

Still, while white Europeans could be assimilated, non-white ethnic groups could not. They could imitate the dominant culture, be judged by its standards and subject to its oppression, but never merge into it. Thus, "ethnicity," in general parlance, has come to refer to those groups which are "unmeltable"—black Americans, Hispanic-Americans, Native Americans, and Asian-Americans.

This is not to suggest that American culture has not been influenced by many racial and cultural groups. A look at the American scene will reveal language, food, music, dances and clothing, among other things, that are aspects of the culture of these ethnic groups. But what finds its way into American culture is carefully chosen and controlled by the dominant white culture. In no sense has the idea of the "melting pot," in which all peoples and cultures are accepted as equal, been realized, though it is one of our favorite images of our destiny A system of isolation, a carefully controlled pattern of the intercourse between and among white and non-white cultures and peoples, and an almost unquestioned myth of white racial and cultural superiority have fostered, nurtured, maintained and encouraged a cultural arrogance which has prevented America from becoming the multi-cultural nation it would be if a more natural development had taken place. A new culture reflecting the many present here would have emerged, as the expressions of the Latin, African, European, Oriental and Native American cultures came into contact with the Anglo-American.

Instead, a cultural arrogance developed, and a sad history of subjugating and exploiting persons who are not part of white culture and the white race within the United States has been written. We have missed the opportunity to enjoy the riches which God has so generously invested in human creation.

It is accurate to say that the increasing "rediscovery" of ethnicity or "ethnic consciousness" by many whites of Southern and Eastern European ancestry has been inspired and influenced by the efforts of the "unmeltable" ethnic groups to recover their heritage and identities. It has also been these "colorful" ethnic groups—and particularly the Black Power and Black Identity movement in the late 60's and the early 70's and the earlier Civil Rights movement, led by Martin Luther King, Jr. and others—that have helped many Anglo-Americans to realize that they, too, are an ethnic group and they are *one* culture among many rather than *the* culture.[13]

In addition, the attempts of ethnic minority groups to seek liberation from oppression have helped a growing number of white middle-class persons to see themselves as oppressed—enslaved to false values, greed, callousness, exploitive powers, and corruption, but also "being oppressed and harassed by many of the same dehumanizing forces of our society that beset those who are not white and middle class." As one very perceptive and stimulating white clergyman has observed: "Under our facades of security, respectability, and righteousness, there lies the reality of our brokenness, our fear, and our uncertainty."[14] Addressing the white middle class, he warns: "White middle class suburbanites need to be liberated as much as anyone else. You and I must consider ourselves oppressed people."[15]

Our cultural arrogance has left us impoverished. It has also left us with a large group of "unmeltable" ethnics who are on the outside of our culture looking in. How, and on what terms, we shall all learn to become *one,* have become urgently pressing questions.

## The "Cultural Mosaic": The Canadian Experience

We need to take a look at the Canadian experience as well, for perhaps at no other point are the similarities and differences between the United States and Canada more easily seen than in this highly sensitive area of intergroup relations.

For one thing, the racial make-up of Canada has been quite different. The Canadian census of 1971 showed that 96.3 percent of Canada's population was of European extraction. Of the balance, 1.4 percent were Indian and Inuit (Eskimo), who together make up the "Native Peoples" of Canada. Another 1.3 percent were Asian, while the remaining 1.0 percent included all those listed as "Others" and "Not Stated." This contrasts markedly with the United States, where, in 1970, 11 percent of the population were black Americans, 3.3 percent were Hispanics, .6 percent were Asians, and .3 percent were Native Americans.

Those whose experience is centered in the United States, and especially the oppressed minorities, tend to see the problem of dominance-subordination in society as essentially a matter of racism. The basic tensions in Canadian life are not between racial groups at all, but between two groups of white Europeans—the Anglos and the French. The Canadian experience reminds us that a dominant group, whether a minority or majority, can—indeed, does—seize upon almost any difference as an excuse for prejudicial treatment of another group. In the Canadian situation, the French had been defeated by British forces on The Plains of Abraham near Quebec City. The Treaty of Paris, signed in 1763, was remarkable for its time in that it granted significant rights to a defeated people. French language and culture, French legal institutions and the Catholic religion were left intact. Nevertheless, over the years the increasing ascendancy of Anglo culture in Canada as a whole has led to resentment and a feeling of being second-class citizens on the part of French-Canadians, while every mandated step to serve French-Canadian interests has built up resistance among Anglo-Canadians. Many French-Canadians would now claim that they have been exploited for political and economic advantage and systematically excluded from full participation in national life. The question whether Quebec will remain within the Canadian confederation—and if so, on what terms—or choose independence—is still open. And that in itself serves to remind us all that the existence of any alienated group within a larger structure can create a crisis at the very heart of the life of any national or cultural entity.

How has this difference in the racial-ethnic background of national life affected relationships among the racial and ethnic minorities in Canada? There has never been an exact Canadian equivalent of the concept of "the melting pot." Instead, Canadians for many years have tended to think of their society as a "cultural mosaic," in which the multicolored elements of Canadian life at once maintained their individual identity and worked together to create the total national image. Finally, in October 1971, Prime Minister Pierre Trudeau declared in the House of Commons that the federal government was adopting a policy of "multiculturalism within a bilingual framework." And this is the official Canadian position today.

One could argue that Canada is ahead of the United States in its treatment of ethnic and religious minorities. As Robert T. Dixon, Superintendent of the Brant County Separate (Roman Catholic) School Board in Ontario, observed, "It is almost an advantage to come from an ethnic group."[16]

One suspects, however, that the multi-cultural path of Canada has its rocky places. The Ontario Ministry of Education, in a guide for use in the preparation of school books, states that words and phrases that generate stereotypes of minority groups should be eliminated. It warns against using hackneyed adjectives as modifiers of ethnic nouns, from "inscrutable" Orientals to "easy-going, fun-loving, rhythmic" West Indians. And it points out that such words as "primitive," "cunning," and "fanatical" may well convey negative values. The very fact that the ministry found it appropriate to issue such a guide provides us with a glimpse into the probable true state of affairs in intergroup relations in that province. And a flurry of letters in the Toronto *Star* early in 1981 demonstrated a lively variety of opinions, in that community at least, as to whether ethnic pluralism is good or bad.

All in all, the Canadian experience adds some important insights into the complexity and ubiquity of the problems of prejudice and ethnic oppression, and affirms the urgent need for developing a truly pluralistic culture.

## Cultural Arrogance and Global Living

Our cultural arrogance has made it all but impossible for us to understand the emerging global community, with its demands for justice and for fundamental changes in our style of life. What does faithfulness to the gospel require of us as we respond to the challenges of a pluralistic society and an interdependent world? How can we help ourselves accept and affirm diversity even when it calls for modifying our attitudes or changing our systems? What risks are inherent in a pluralistic society? What is necessary to help us enjoy and celebrate diversity with a new awareness, and to find the confidence to participate fully in a pluralistic society?

There is no doubt in anyone's mind that we live in global community. Through vast technological and scientific developments and especially by means of the mass media and mass transportation facilities, all areas of the globe have been linked together, giving us the means of living, participating and being present in the *whole* world. International travel facilities to all major foreign cities make it possible to reach all continents and most countries in a matter of hours and in a good deal of comfort. Domestic airlines within those countries make it possible for passengers to reach remote areas, even in countries in the process of modern development.

Radio and television instantly leap the barriers of geography, language, politics and distance, sending messages and information across the world. A worldwide network of relay satellites allows for instantaneous television reportage of what is happening in the world. Words and pictures of war, revolution, international catastrophes, political elections and other events are reported in a split second to the world community.

To speak of world community amid the conflicts and tensions of our times is, in some sense, ludicrous. On the other hand, every day brings fresh evidence that the world of earth is rapidly becoming one community, with or without the oneness of "community"—a

59

"global village" in which the interests of corporations and nation-states affect the welfare of persons in other parts of the world in significant ways. We are part of a new kind of global reality, participants in common, identifiable global experiences.

John Donne wrote, "No man is an island," and cautioned, "never send to know for whom the bell tolls; it tolls for thee." In today's global community, the bell most often tolls far out of earshot. As the Third World demands freedom and justice, the conditions of global living add significance to our perception of ourselves as citizens of the world and our participation in the worldwide Christian church, which is supra-national, multi-ethnic and economically diverse in character. The emerging nations of Asia, Africa and Latin America and their quest for independent self-rule, human dignity and power, their cries of protest against the trans-national elites whose international mechanisms and structures of economic systems exploit them, are heard around the globe.

The old distinction between "national" and "international" no longer holds as we face the pressure of today's global realities. While this is not a new fact, it is a more pressing one than ever to be reckoned with, and its far-reaching implications are more immediate. During the depression of the 30's, for example, few were aware that a lockout in Gadsden, Alabama, rubber plants might be responsible for the pawning of loincloths in Bali. In 1973, we all understood that the Arab oil embargo confronted Americans and Western Europeans with the hard realities of the interdependence of highly developed technological societies and the nearby developing Third World nations. An increase in the cost of a barrel of oil from Kuwait affects the price of a gallon of gasoline in Kansas.

In short, these global realities place upon us an unprecedented demand for change. A new understanding of our identity is required. Effective educational programs will be needed to help persons of the dominant cultural group participate with other cultural and national groupings to create a just world community. An adequate theology for living in a global community must be developed. An effort must be made to search for values and lifestyles that are not oppressive, but just. With renewed intentionality and conscientization we necessarily must seek awareness of those forces which objectify, dehumanize and oppress, and must search out new ways of overcoming them.[17] "For in our shrinking globe we can ill-afford illiteracy."[18]

# Cultural Arrogance and Emerging Pluralism

Cultural arrogance has made it difficult for us to recognize the truth about ourselves and about our situation: the process of assimilation has betrayed the American dream of "the melting pot." It has left us confronted at home by what have come to be called "the unmeltable ethnics": a numerical majority, in total, which rejects the claim of the minority whites to dominant status. It has left us confronted in the global community by a rising tide of expectations on the part of the Third World: a numerical majority which is increasingly impatient with our cultural inability to produce the real leadership that dominant status requires.

## The Vacuum at the Center

After exercising leadership for many years and dominating society's values and institutions, the elite has greatly diminished in influence during the recent decades. "After having *been* the society, the Protestants have been relegated to *a place* within the society, and increasingly they experience a bewildering sense of themselves as a new minority."[19] Some have acknowledged this decline but cannot foresee where it will end; "in relation to other American ethnic, cultural, and religious groups they do not know their place."[20] Many others "have *not yet faced* the fact of the decline itself, much less its consequences."[21] The decline involves a group of persons who traditionally not only claimed "the most secure identity and status in America," but also served as "guardian of our social hierarchy, assigning other groups to their proper stations."[22] According to Greenbaum, this decline in leadership was due first of all to excessive materialism, as Alexis de Tocqueville and Max Weber had concluded before him. But Greenbaum singled out three additional factors as well, each stemming from the leadership's distance from the whole of the society: "(1) the Protestants' usurpation of legitimacy; (2) their failure to resolve basic value contradictions; and (3) their overreliance on the paradigm of science and technology."[23] The resulting decline of Protestant domination has left the United States without an ideal toward which the socialization process can be directed.[24]

## New Resources for Unity

In the place of the old ideal, now discredited, Greenbaum calls for support of pluralistic institutions and communities and setting policies that honor diversity as a way of maintaining unity, while developing a new, universal ideal.

Greenbaum believes that new ideals must draw on "more diverse cultural, social, economic and political models than those provided by the Anglo-Saxon, Western European, Anglo-American tradition."[25] For alternative ideals we must look to ethnic groups who have known different values. "We must learn from Native Americans, Chicanos, Puerto Ricans, blacks, Chinese and other oppressed groups both here and throughout the Third World."[26] Arguing that these groups have the least vested in materialism, he proposes that *"the past exclusion of minority and Third World people from the Western mainstream may turn out to be humanity's greatest hope."*

Greenbaum's proposal calls us to "honor alternative worth, to revive and reconsider subordinated alternative values, and to create new, self-respecting institutions and communities."[27] If these minority and Third World peoples throughout the world can receive "magnanimous respect in the proportions that the Protestant Anglo-American majority deserves pity," Greenbaum believes we can together find a new universal human ideal. He warns that the task will be difficult and complicated, especially for the declined Protestant majority, who must learn to cope with guilt as they increasingly learn to respect those who have descended from the people they have for centuries treated as inhuman. Such an undertaking will require us "to extend ourselves to listen to those at the margins, where throughout history mankind's prophets have been found."[28]

E. Digsby Baltzell, in his study of the decline of Protestant leadership in America entitled *The Protestant Establishment*, starts from a different point of view, but develops a similar argument. He renders his criticism constructively, though with regret: "A crisis in moral authority has developed in modern America, largely because of the White-Anglo-Saxon Protestant establishment's unwillingness, or inability, to share and improve its upper-class traditions by continuously absorbing talented and distinguished members of minority groups into its privileged ranks."[29]

Greenbaum has succintly stated what he sees as the contradictions in the values and ideals of the Protestant Anglo-American culture that have not been resolved and that, when unresolved, preclude a new sense of purpose:

- equality and justice in tension with rights of private property;
- individualism mocked by two of its outcomes in a capitalist state—insecurity and conformity;
- respect for religious affiliation and disdain for orthodox religion;
- reliance on the strength of the American family and on high rates of social, occupational and residential mobility that tear families apart;
- respect for craft coupled with respect for high speed;
- agrarian values in conflict with industrialization and urbanization;
- self-restraint offset by ravenous materialism;
- dependence on inquiry and self-criticism and sanctions against the same;
- belief with Luther that religion should be above church and state and that politics is a lower form of activity versus belief with Calvin that Protestantism includes responsibility for systematically reordering the world in all of its religious, economic, and political aspects; and
- faith in a republican form of government and legitimate usurpation coupled with encouragement of broad expectations regarding democracy and equality of opportunity.[30]

It was these unresolved contradictions that prevented America from becoming truly pluralistic in actuality. It is these contradictions that still must be resolved. In spite of its attempt to create a sanctuary for those who left their experience of misrule in Europe, the United States turned out to be, on closer examination, what Milton Gordon calls "the clubhouse of a particular ethnic group—the white Anglo-Saxon Protestants, its operations shot through with the premises and expectations of its parental ethnicity." Doors that appeared to be open were in fact closed to certain ethnic groups. Invisible barriers in the corporate structure and other places of privilege and power proved to be impenetrable.

No group was made more painfully and dramatically aware of these closed doors than black Americans. The history of harsh and brutal exclusion and the accompanying exploitation and oppression is one of the saddest chapters of American history. And the chapter is not finished. The black experience of white coercion, violence, exclusion and unconscious projection of frustration onto black intention are unparalleled in the republic. Exposed to the exalted notion of success, lured by the rhetoric of freedom, justice and equality, and converted to a religion which preached the oneness of man, blacks found themselves defined by the culture as less than persons. Harold

Cruse has described the failure of the nation to resolve this contradiction, and the cultural crisis to which it has brought us:

America is an unfinished nation—the product of a badly-bungled process of inter-group cultural fusion. America is a nation that lies to itself about who and what it is. It is a nation of minorities ruled by a minority of one—it thinks and acts as if it were a nation of white Anglo-Saxon Protestants. The white Anglo-Saxon ideal, this lofty dream of a minority at the summit of its economic and political power and the height of its historical self-delusions, has led this nation to the brink of self-destruction. And on its way, *it has effectively dissuaded, crippled and smothered the cultivation of a democratic cultural pluralism in America*. The cultural mainstream of the nation is an empty street, full of bright lights that try to glamorize the *cultural wreckage and flotsam* of our times.[31]

## The Coming Revolution

One may disagree with Cruse's belief that the solution to our difficulty lies in "revolutionizing the administration, the organization, the functioning and the social purpose of the entire American apparatus of cultural communication and placing it under public ownership," but one cannot deny his recognition that those who control the image-making capacity of the nation's media maintain the order of social reality. Any lasting change depends upon an alteration of the people's view of social reality. This means a radical reorientation in human consciousness. Clearly, what Cruse's proposal calls for is a "revolution of values," to use the phrase of Martin Luther King, Jr.

What Cruse, Greenbaum and Baltzell share is a recognition that we are at a point of crisis in culture and cultural identity. Many previously held values, roles, behaviors and institutions have been discredited and can no longer function as the unifying centers or the sole sources for the transformation of society. The times demand no less than a revolution in consciousness. The American dream has been devoured by a ravenous reality—the Anglo-American ideals of culture must give way to a pluralism that allows for genuine diversity, to a more broadly based and universal ideal, to a cultural and racial pluralism in which there is respect for and appreciation of differences, and to institutions that are influenced and shaped by much more diverse cultural, social, economic, religious and political models than those provided by the white Anglo-American, Western European tradition.

# CHAPTER 3: RECALL/RESPONSE

## RECALL

"If [our cultural biases, values, beliefs, attitudes, behaviors, lifestyles and expectations of others] are not effectively challenged by exposure to varied ways of life and by diverse relationships, and are not confronted by a plurality of competing views, norms or definitions of reality ... then a kind of 'parochial self-absorption' develops. ... Others whose cultures may differ from ours, or persons of racial and ethnic groups different from ours, are evaluated or scaled in reference to our group. ... Unless the whole sociocultural context can be challenged and a new understanding of the place of our own culture among other cultures emerges, individuals and structures continue to operate within a web of social norms and restraints that become oppressive and set limits on our freedom and the freedom of others."

"Cultural arrogance deprives the dominating group of human interrelating with other cultures, of the beauty, values and richness to be experienced in other cultures, and of the enriched appreciation for their own deeper cultural values that can emerge from awareness of the cultures of others. ... Cultural deprivation is the price cultural arrogance forces us to pay."

## RESPONSE

(1) How one views another culture is influenced and perhaps determined by how one views one's own culture. Compare the

following three models and discuss how a particular event, issue or task will be viewed in the light of each model.

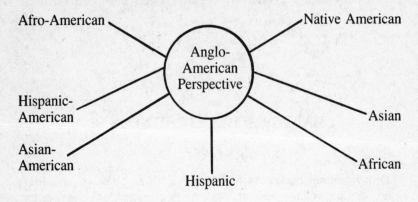

*MODEL A:* Anglo-American perspective is central. There is a tendency to feel that Anglo-American culture is superior to all others, exists at the center of the universe, and that all others should be scaled and graded with reference to it.

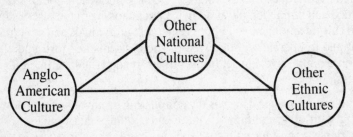

*MODEL B:* The Anglo-American culture is only one of several cultures and is in no way superior or inferior to other ethnic or national perspectives.

*MODEL C:* Two or more cultures are mutual partners engaged in a shared experience of learning and action.

(2) Values differ from culture to culture. The Value Classification chart (Table 8) included here reveals the relative weight placed on specific values in the major cultures of the world. What does this survey suggest in terms of our experience of other cultures of the world. What does this survey suggest in terms of our experience of other cultures? Take a few values such as gratefulness, money, individuality, respect for elders, authority, efficiency and discuss them in the light of different cultures. In what ways do these and the assumptions we make about these values confuse our understanding of the demands of the gospel and our own cultural norms?

(3) An Asian-American is being considered for the position of youth minister for your church. His credentials are excellent by all standards. He is invited to an interview with the personnel committee of your congregation, but he is not offered the job. Later you hear that the reason he did not get the job is that "he is too quiet." Most of the membership of your youth group agree with this decision because they need someone who is gregarious and has a winsome personality. Yet, in the Chinese culture, quietness and respect for superiors is considered an important value; thus when the Chinese-American was purposefully quiet in the interview, the personnel committee misinterpreted this quietness as incompetence and nonassertiveness. If a similar situation should occur, what suggestions could you make to (a) the Chinese-American? (b) the personnel committee?

# TABLE 8

## Value Classification System

| Value | Primary | Secondary | Tertiary | Negligible |
|---|---|---|---|---|
| Individuality | W | B | E | M |
| Motherhood | BE | MW | – | – |
| Hierarchy | WEMA | B | – | – |
| Masculinity | BMEWA | – | – | – |
| Gratefulness | EA | MB | W | – |
| Peace | E | B | WA | M |
| Money | WAB | M | E | – |
| Modesty | E | BAM | – | W |
| Punctuality | W | B | ME | A |
| Saviorism | W | M | – | EBM |
| Karma | E | – | – | MWBA |
| Firstness | W | B | – | EAM |
| Aggressiveness | WB | M | AE | – |
| Collective Responsibility | EAM | B | – | W |
| Respect for Elders | EAM | B | – | W |
| Respect for Youth | W | MABE | – | – |
| Hospitality to Guests | EA | B | MW | – |
| Inherited Property | E | – | MWAB | – |
| Preservation of Environment | E | BA | W | M |
| Color of Skin | EWB | M | – | A |
| Sacredness of Farm Land | E | A | – | BMW |
| Equality of Women | W | EB | A | M |
| Human Dignity | WB | EAM | – | – |
| Efficiency | W | B | EM | – |
| Patriotism | BMAE | W | – | – |
| Religion | WBMAE | – | – | – |
| Authoritarianism | EMA | WB | – | – |
| Education | WB | EAM | – | – |
| Frankness | W | BEMA | – | – |

Legend— W = Western cultures    A = African cultures
        E = Eastern cultures    M = Muslim cultures
        B = Black cultures

(4) The January 3, 1981, issue of the *Toronto Star* reported that the Ontario Ministry of Education issued a guide for publishing textbooks eliminating derogatory references to non-whites, such as "easy-going, fun-loving, rhythmic" West Indians, "inscrutable" Orientals and "people from darkest Africa." Such descriptive terms as "primitive," "cunning," "fanatical," "poor and overpopulated" were seen to convey negative values by innuendo. Can you think of other examples of such negative values suggested by innuendo in writing about ethnic groups? Develop a list of such negative terms and then in a second column create positive alternatives. Show why one is negative and the other positive.

(5) E. Digsby Baltzell, in his study of the decline of Protestant leadership in America *(The Protestant Establishment)* cited in Chapter 3, maintains that "A crisis in moral authority has developed in modern America, largely because of the White-Anglo-Saxon Protestant establishment's unwillingness, or inability, to share and improve its upper-class traditions by continuously absorbing talented and distinguished members of minority groups into its privileged ranks." Can you cite specific examples in which ethnic groups and their contributions could make a difference? Do you think it is still possible? If not, why not?

(6) Very often we confuse our values in a given culture with the requirements of the gospel. We then make judgments about others based on how closely they approximate our "standards." Divide into smaller groups. Each group is to develop a biblical and/or theological basis for their understanding of:
—time
—play
—work
—privacy
—success
—sex roles

The smaller groups may then report to the whole study group on the "results" of their theologizing, with the opportunity for challenges from the other small groups.

(7) We as North Americans are undergoing a crisis of culture identity, and previous anchors (rules, values, roles, etc.) are giving way to new choices. How are you affected *personally?*
 —at home
 —at work/school
 —at church
 —in your community

# 4

# THEOLOGICAL AND BIBLICAL FOUNDATIONS FOR PLURALISM

It is an axiom of the Christian faith that all humankind is one family. In the acts of grace in creation and redemption God has made humankind into a unity of destiny and dignity. God's continuing presence in nature and in history gives us a sense of identity and purpose from which we derive our oneness and our humanity. In the words of the Uppsala Report of 1968: "Mankind is understood as a whole, with a common nature (created from one head), with common problems (sin, suffering, death), with a common future (the Kingdom of God, for every nation, people and tongue; the uniting of all things in Christ) and with a common calling (to faith, love and hope.)"[1] The world is one people.

## The Sin of Racism

For too long the Christian church has dealt with racism as if it were simply a moral problem, a social transgression or a matter of inadequate knowledge. Racism is at its deepest and most fundamental level a theological problem. As important and helpful as the factual and moral data are, they simply help us to place in perspective the deeper and ultimate perversities of will that are at the heart of the final demonic inequity—the worship of the finite. Put simply, racism is sin.

*Racism is sin because it divides the human family and blurs the image of God in human persons.* We are created in the image of God. We possess as creatures of God what the theologians call the *imago dei*—the image of God. This means that God has bestowed upon each individual the mark of God, made that person in the divine image and called that person to a common human destiny. God alone is the source of human dignity. Therein we find our likeness to God. It is not an achievement or a merit or even an intrinsic quality; it is a gift; it is conferred.

God has bestowed on all humans an equal degree of humanity, potentiality for the spiritual, and an equal amount of human dignity. This is the basis for the essential unity of humankind, for our likeness to God and our likeness to one another. This understanding, from a biblical perspective, is not based on empirical evidence, though modern science provides it, but from faith in God as the Creator and in the nature of that creation. As Emil Brunner, the late Swiss theologian, put it:

> The religious belief in the unity of the human race through the Creation, in and for the Divine image, is completely independent of all biological, palaeontological, scientific results. The story of Adam in Genesis expresses, in historical form, it is true, a fact which in itself is super-empirical and super-historical; the biological, genealogical question has very little to do with belief in the unity of the creation. . . . The unity of the divine creation of man lies upon a quite different plane. Humanity is not necessarily a unity from a zoological point of view; it may indeed be composed of different species of differing origin or it may not. It is, however, beyond all doubt a unity, a *humanitas,* through the *humanum,* its one origin and its one destiny in God's creative Word and plan of salvation, spiritually given to man by God himself.[2]

To divide what God has made as a unity and to blur that image by judging and separating persons by the color of their skin, to blur it by denying persons the human dignity bestowed by God, is to commit sin against God and God's creation. Racism does exactly that.

*Racism is sin because it worships the finite. It replaces God with race.* The racist elevates skin color to an ultimate value, to the highest category for valuing human lives. Instead of worshipping God, the source of being, and expressing thanks for the grace of God in which the image of God is rooted and grounded, the racist replaces the image of God with the image of self. Superiority over other races is assumed. Purity, wisdom, virtue, creativity, uncontaminated genetic structure and unmixed essence are likewise assumed, and are assumed to apply only to those who are like the racist in skin color. All others are inferior.

Thus racists engage in self-deification, self-glorification and unthankful arrogance. Thus racists reject the divine sovereign and set themselves up as the measure of all things. Racial pride becomes the center of the action. Skin color becomes the criterion for love, value and worth, and devotion to God is replaced by devotion to racial/racist values. As Waldo Beach observed:

> From the standpoint of classical Christian thought, of course, racial prejudice is not one of a catalogue of sins, but is a facet or expression of the single sin of "pride," the rejection of the Infinite Sovereign Source of life and the attempt to set up as final some substitute sovereignty derived from the finite. In so far as fallen, man tends to make of himself...the center of love and value. Racial pride within and discriminatory practices are one ready way among many to "exchange the truth of God for a lie," and to worship "the creature rather than the Creator."[3]

Racists look to race as the source of their personal value. "The God of racism is the race, the ultimate center of value," as George Kelsey has pointed out.[4] Race becomes the decisive point of reference for decisions and action. Public policies and institutions, private life, social intercourse, marriage and family, neighborhood, and even religious institutions are organized upon the foundation of race. Race becomes the idol that determines attitudes, decisions and actions. God, the Christian faith, democracy, morality, the teachings of Jesus, Buddha or Mohammed—all such sources of values—are subordinated to the god of race.

The racists are not simply the hooded members of the Ku Klux Klan who burn crosses and murder and pillage. They are law-abiding citizens who would be horror-struck by cross burnings. They are church members who attend regularly and give generously. They are Protestants, Catholics and Jews, Southerners and Northerners, rich and poor, white and black, old and young. While the racists may not recognize it, a review of their lives, their decisions and the pattern of their actions will reveal the true source of their sense of personal value. They are any who rely upon race for their sense of worth and who substitute race for God as the ultimate determiner in their lives.

Racism boasts of its ability to stay on top, but in actuality the boasting is the sound of fear—that the stage of history will shift so sharply that the racists' methods of extermination and domination of their alleged inferiors will no longer prevail. For the prospect of a world without racism is a threatening thought.

Isaac Bivens of the Board of Global Ministries of The United Methodist Church tells of an incident that occurred in this country during the turbulent 60's; it is a good—and disturbing—illustration of this psychology. It took place in a community that was caught up in the struggle for school integration. A parent had been deeply involved in the issue because she did not want her children going to school with black children. One day her little girl came home very dejected. The child had obviously been crying. Her mother asked her, "What happened to you today?" After some sobbing and pouting, the little girl said she was upset because Mary Lou had left her school that day. Mary Lou was the only black girl in the school. Her mother was rather disappointed and surprised. "Why should you be sad because Mary Lou is not in school any more?" she asked. "Mother," the little girl said, "Mary Lou is the only girl in that school that I'm better than."

The racists' euphoria, their self-confidence, and their very reason to be are based upon the presupposition that they are inherently better than "them." This gives them identity. This is the thing that links them to the success syndrome of a white-dominated society. Like the little girl, they need someone to be better than.

Racial domination over other racial and ethnic groups is not always blatant. It is sometimes subtle and even takes the form of paternalistic love. Looking only on the face of this form of racism, one could almost call it Christian charity. But when one looks deeper one can see the subterranean streams of racism flowing.

The respectable, cultured form of racial pride is exactly this paternalistic love, the concern of the superior for the inferior. The Negro neighbor is loved, is cared for. Thus, in the eyes of the paternalist and churchman the law of Christ is fulfilled in his [sic] own behavior. His very kindness is an aid to self-deceit. He is blinded to the corruption at the heart of paternalistic love: that the neighbor is loved, not by reference to God the Creator, but by reference to the sinful order of white superiority and Negro inferiority. The neighbor is loved only in so far as he understands the terms of the transaction and "keeps his place." Thus,

74

the mutual love of the order of creation is poisoned at its font by self-love. The resultant paternalism is a disorder of God's basic order of created community.[5]

The racists relate on the basis of power, not love; domination, not equality; superiority, not sisterhood or brotherhood. Even in performing "acts of kindness," the racists must be on top and must be sure the victims recognize that. In so doing, the racists are "reaching down" to an inferior and not "reaching across" to a neighbor—a fellow creature who has been imprinted with the stamp of God.

*Racism is sin because it calls into question God's creation and makes a pejorative judgment concerning God's action.*[6] One of the implications of racism is that God made a mistake in creating races other than the white race. Since the other races are defective and inferior, the racists consign them to a lower status and consider them destined to be the permanent victims of history and ultimately without hope. They are without hope, from the Christian racists' perspective, because their "fall" is a second, racial "fall" from grace, in which there is no promise of renewal and redemption, and they must forever be the "hewers of the wood and the drawers of the water." Thus the racists "rectify" God's "error."

A related perspective on this sin is that racists simply fail to acknowledge that all of what God made in the act of creation is good.

*Racism is sin because it violates God's will.* For members of the Christian community, the supreme source of duty is the will of God. The will of God is found in Jesus, his teachings, and his incarnation. Jesus taught that God requires a wholehearted response to God and a wholehearted love for our neighbor. In fact, he made this the summary of the law of God. Where that law is broken, our covenant with God is fractured. We then live in sin.

Racism is disobedience to the law of love. It is not merely a disregard for the teachings of Jesus; it is a blatant denial of the truth Jesus lived and taught, i.e., that we are all brothers and sisters in one family. It is a refusal to see that we all bear the imprint of the Creator and are enlivened by the breath of one Spirit and reconciled and redeemed by the work of Jesus Christ. As the Fourth Assembly of the World Council of Churches in Uppsala stated it: "Racism is a blatant denial of the Christian faith. It denies the effectiveness of the reconciling work of Jesus Christ, through whose love all human diversities lose their divisive significance."[7]

# Pluralism and the Law of Love

While few would argue with the accuracy of the scriptural commandment to love, racists simply deny—in their attitudes, actions, decisions and lives—that this revelation of the will of God applies to their relationship to persons who differ from them in color, culture, custom and belief. In point of fact, they answer the lawyer's question "Who is my neighbor?" differently than Jesus did.[8] Jesus was quite clear that *all* persons are our neighbors. No one is excluded. Every person's place in existence becomes ours, even the non-Christian's. Every person is a "thou" because he or she is a creature of God.

The law of love does not allow Christians to set their own conditions for their obedience. The law is absolute. The bases for Christian relating to others are set, not by conditions which pertain to others—their color, their class, their culture, their vice or virtue, their place of origin, their belief system, their worthiness or unworthiness—but by the radical nature of the demand of the law of Christ. Christ, not the other person, determines the Christian's response, attitude and behavior. When the individual Christian stops "desiring to justify himself" (Luke 10:29) and sees Christ as the "compassionate neighbor," then he or she becomes the recipient of God's love; it is then possible to love God and one's neighbors.[9]

This love of neighbor is not merely sentimental infatuation with the idea of love. Love is not sheer condescending emotion to satisfy religious piety; it is not pity directed toward the poor or those in need. Love is not love if there is not acceptance of the other person's grief, worth, suffering, humiliation and hope. The love that the Master talked about, and was the embodiment of in his own person and work, was not rarefied abstraction or a sentimental idea. God acted concretely in Jesus Christ. The man Jesus "'reveals God's love by what he says, does and is.'"[10]

Our love for God and for the neighbor means joining God in concrete action in the world, and more often than not, this involves power and justice. As Paul Tillich pointed out: "Love is the foundation, not the negation of power."[11] Tillich insisted that love, power and justice are inseparable. "Love and power are often contrasted in such a way that love is identified with a resignation of power and power with a denial of love. *Powerless love* and *loveless power* are contrasted. This, of course, is unavoidable if love is understood from

76

its emotional side and power from its compulsory side. But such an understanding is error and confusion."[12] The white racists forget about the interrelatedness of these concepts, and when they express an effort of "love" toward non-whites at all, it is the "powerless love" of sentimentality and emotions—a sure way of making those receiving it into non-persons.

Christian love is to will that every person may grow to the fullest and enjoy the "abundant life." But it goes further. It is the willingness to take specific and concrete action so that what is willed may be realized. In individual relationships this means meeting any person as a thou rather than an it. Applied to the context of oppression: Christian love requires that the oppressed cannot allow themselves to be addressed as things; the oppressors need radically to alter their attitudes, perceptions and behavior and relate to those oppressed as persons.[13] In other words, Christian love requires a move to equalize the relationship. As one friend of mine insists: "Profound love can only exist between two equals."[14]

In a society, as distinguished from an individual relationship, Christian love requires the establishment of justice. This means correcting structures of society so that all of its members are provided the opportunity to develop to their fullest capacities. It means removing the distortions that prevent that development. Love addresses the inequities and injustices that obstruct the relationships of groups to one another and the establishment of a just society to perpetuate such love.

Although he writes from the perspective of secular psychiatry, Erich Fromm can teach us much about genuine Christian love. In describing *biophilia*, the love of life, Fromm says, "Love for life will develop most in a society where there is: *security* in the sense that the basic material conditions for a dignified life are not threatened, *justice* in the sense that nobody can be an end for the purposes of another, and *freedom* in the sense that each man [sic] has the possibility to be an active and responsible member of society."[15] What Fromm is suggesting is that love requires active justice. Christians must translate love into specific acts of justice and power.

And there's the rub. Racism fails to express genuine Christian love because it stereotypes and marginalizes whole segments of the population whose presence it perceives as a threat. Minority poor are seen as the dross and burden of a post-industrial society—without skills, without motivation, without incentive and therefore expendable in our highly developed technological and computerized society. Having served their function as cheap labor, they are no longer useful. The blatant exploitation of persons as instruments for gain gives way to a callous indifference. Open hatred and crude and blatant expressions of vulgar racial epithets have been replaced with a more-often-than-not sophisticated but cynical and sinister silent neglect.

Middle- and upper-class non-whites are not exempt from the effects and consequences of racism. In spite of the "illusion of progress"[16] promoted by those who are card-carrying members of the "White Male Club,"[17] redlining, discrimination in hiring, housing discrimination, a lack of distinction between wealth and income,[18] reactionary attitudes and responses toward Affirmative Action, ghetto-ization of non-white ethnic groups and myriads of other heinous effects of racism spread the insidious tentacles of white power into the lives of non-whites daily.

This racism has a new face. It is the face of computer printouts, of nameless statistics, of graphs of profits and losses, of invisible minorities, of pink slips, of the fingerprinted record and the stencilled number of a prison uniform.

The sin of racism stalks our land and haunts our society. It mocks the words of Jesus: "So whatever you wish that men would do to you, do so to them" (Matt. 7:12) and blurs the vision of the One who said, "As you did it to one of the least of these my brethren, you did it to me" (Matt. 25:40).

## Creation and Equality

The Christian doctrine of creation maintains that it is in the act of creation itself that equality is achieved.[19] We are not beings of ourselves and for ourselves; we are dependent beings. We owe our existence to God. It is in God we live and move and have our being. Our rights and our claims and our transcendent worth are based on God's act in creation. As Bultmann says:

> It means, first of all, that we are creatures, that we are dust and ashes, and that in ourselves we are nothing. It means that in ourselves we have no permanence, and nothing whereupon we could base our own right and our own claims, nothing that we ourselves can assert as the meaning and worth of our life.[20]

We do not have our own life at our disposal, nor do we have the lives of other persons. We are creatures who share an essential unity in creation. Our humanity derives from an act of grace in creation—a gift of conferred dignity.

When man[sic] enters into the love of God revealed in Christ he becomes truly human. True human existence is existence in the love of God. . . . True humanity is not genius but love, that love which man does not possess from or in himself but which he receives from God, who is love. True humanity does not spring from the full development of human potentialities, but it arises through the reception, the perception, and the acceptance of the love of God, and it develops and is preserved by "abiding" in communion with the God who reveals Himself as Love.[21]

Equality is not based on achievement or merit. Equality does not suggest that all persons are equal in intelligence, capacity, skill, knowledge or talent. Few of us have the eloquence of Martin Luther King, Jr., or the genius of Albert Einstein or the talent of Shirley Verrett. Equality means that persons can claim equal rights as persons, as creatures of God made in God's image. These are rights that belong to all persons, merely by virtue of their being persons created in the image of God, who share a unity and a destiny as God's sons and daughters. This right exists prior to any achievement, merit or performance of any function. It is a basic and primary right—an "inalienable right," as recognized by the framers of the American Declaration of Independence, though of course it existed long, long before they put it into words for the new nation. It is part of the order of creation. It is an imperative of love from the Creator.

The framers of the Declaration of Independence, in stating "All men are created equal," were writing into a democratic political document a statement of truth that the biblical faith had discovered and even dogmatized centuries before: "And he made from one every nation of men to live on all the face of the earth" (Acts 17:26).

The Christian religion bases its concept of equality on God's act of creation. Persons are sacred through God and because they are imprinted with God's image. There are no degrees or scales of human worth. Our sacredness in our particularity or individuality is secondary. What is primary is that God has made us, sustained us, chastised and forgiven us, loved us, sought us, and in the ultimate gracious act at Calvary completed a mysterious transaction of suffering and salvation for us. It is through faith in such a God as this that we stake our claim for human dignity and equality.

We cannot claim the sacredness of any person until we acknowledge the sacredness of all persons; our dignity and holiness are not in us except as they are in our Maker. We can look upon any person—the profligate as well as the priest, the sinner as well as the saint, the rat-bitten child of the ghetto as well as the clean-scrubbed private-school student—and know that in that person, however blurred, blotted or blemished by circumstance, we are looking at the image of the Eternal God. The sacredness of human persons, the infinite worth of human personality, has nothing to do with color, intellect, culture, race, morality, faith or anything else; it has to do with God, who created all persons and placed a God-stamp on them and a God-destined likeness in them. To deny any persons dignity, to deny any persons equality by our acts and structures of racism, oppression, cultural degradation and exclusion, is to be in conflict with God—the very essence of sin.

Many individuals prefer to see acts of racism and the accompanying evils of poverty, ethnic oppression, economic exploitation and cultural imperialism as matters outside the purview of their personal concern. While they may accept equality as, in general, a good thing, they lack a sense of the monstrosity of inequality, and the urgency of the imperative for justice. They fail to see the widening gap between the incomes of whites and non-whites in this country, the great discrepancy between unemployment in the black and Hispanic communities and unemployment in the white community, the steady and constant erosion of quality education in urban schools and the growing rate of urban crime fed and fostered by deteriorating social conditions.

The failure to see this gap leads to indifference to evil, inequality and injustice. Indifference prefers to remain neutral, impartial and unmoved by the extremity of these evils, and dismisses as platitudes any calls to concern and action. Such indifference to evil is even more insidious than evil itself; it is more widespread, more contagious and far more dangerous. To be silent and unconcerned gives tacit justification to these evils. It makes it possible for these evils, which erupt as exceptions, to become in time the rule—and to be accepted as such. Indifferent persons are decent but sinister, pious but nevertheless sinful. Problems that should be regarded as a scandal to the human heart are seen instead as social conditions evolving predictably from "the way things are."

Part of the problem is that most of the majority population perceives justice and equality as the ideals, as fine social *goals*—good if obtained, but essentially a utopian idea. But in the eyes of the prophets and in the eyes of Jesus, justice was not a pot of gold at the end of a rainbow. This is not what the eighth-century prophet Amos had in mind when he thundered: "Let justice roll down like waters, and righteousness like an ever-flowing stream" (Amos 5:24). Justice is a mighty stream, with the vehemence of never-ending, surging, fighting movement—washing away obstacles as its mighty waters roll down. "But the mountain falls and crumbles away, and the rock is removed from its place; the waters wear away the stones" (Job 14:18ff). No, justice is not merely a utopian idea, a desirable norm, but a restless drive empowered by an omnipotent God. As the prophets saw it: What ought to be, must be!

## The Meaning of Pluralism

What is the nature of the pluralism we seek? For our purpose here, "pluralism" is used to mean a condition in society in which members of diverse ethnic, racial, religious and social groups maintain autonomous participation in and development of their own traditional culture or specific interests within the confines of a common society and form of government. It means an unwillingness on the part of these ethnic, racial and social groups to sacrifice their own identity, history, ideas, memories, sentiments, aspirations, values and social and cultural styles for the sake of the dominant white, Western European tradition. It does not refer simply to the variety of such things as exotic recipes, colorful costumes and folk dances (although these may be a part of it), but includes interaction among such significant intangibles as values, ways of looking at life and the world, diverse traditions and ideas; the impact that minority groups are having on the redistribution of political power; the extension of civil rights; a different interpretation of history; and the more direct, positive meaning in individuals' lives that results from pluralistic thinking. Pluralism means realizing, affirming and appreciating an extraordinary diversity among us in the same place.

The racial and cultural pluralism in the Christian church reflects the same diversity present in the larger community—to be realized, affirmed and appreciated. And the church encompasses the dynamic of another kind of diversity—diversity in religious opinion and in interpretation of the Christian call. How does a group that is bound by a common faith deal with its differences within? How do we regard the boundaries of the sub-groups within "the tie that binds"?

Pluralism means that dogmatists and their dogma hold a place as well as the open-minded and their postulates; the conservatives as well as the liberals, the evangelicals (on the right or left) and the social activists (on the left or right) have a place. But no *special* place. Until we can allow others to be themselves without requiring them to pay a dreadful price, and can allow ourselves the freedom to be ourselves without arrogant egotism, it is impossible to love another human being truly.

Pluralism brings into sharp focus the necessary and creative tension between similarity and difference. It provides genuine options, variety, diverse centers of power and self-determination. In the words of Michael Novak, it "recognizes that no one set of social pressures is sufficent to inspire the full range of human possibilities."[22]

Ethnic pluralism provides an affirmation of ethnic variety which enriches all groups and traditions. It is not universality accomplished by extension of Anglo-American Protestant values and culture to establish a super mono-culture, but is built upon the broad base of all the ethnic cultures. It is based upon the assumption that a society is greatly enriched by diversity and that such a society experiences creativity and growth because of the presence of such variety in its life.

# CHAPTER 4: RECALL/RESPONSE

## RECALL

"The law of love does not allow Christians to set their own conditions for their obedience. The law is absolute. The bases for Christian relating to others are set, not by conditions which pertain to others—their color, their class, their culture, their vice or virtue, their place of origin, their belief system, their worthiness or unworthiness—but by the radical nature of the demand of the law of Christ."

"We cannot claim the sacredness of any person until we acknowledge the sacredness of all persons; our dignity and holiness are not in us except as they are in our Maker. We can look upon any person... and know that in that person, however blurred, blotted or blemished by circumstance, we are looking at the image of the Eternal God. The sacredness of human persons, the infinite worth of human personality, has nothing to do with color, intellect, culture, race, morality, faith or anything else; it has to do with God, who created all persons and place a God-stamp on them and a God-destined likeness in them."

## RESPONSE

(1) Your local church is concerned because it doesn't have any contact with the Hispanic church in the Spanish neighborhood. Since your church is a well-to-do church with a surplus of funds and the Hispanic church is poor, the decision is made to offer some financial aid as an initial way of establishing contact and also a responsible way to use the excess funds. Contact is made with the officers and pastor of the Hispanic church, indicating your church's desire to carry out this decision. However, the Hispanic church rejects the offer. The Hispanic spokesperson says, "We reject your money and see it as an act of charity and token aid. It is a substitute for justice and a paternalistic act on your part." What, now, is the response of your church? Plan your further actions in specifics. Answer the questions raised in your own minds by this rejection. There is, of course, the possibility of "shaking the dust from your feet."

(2) Aside from ethnic foods (pizza, egg rolls, etc.), discuss concrete examples of how different cultures impact upon *your* life.

(3) A group of social activists are criticizing church A as being too "biblical" and "churchy." Says one: "We need to be serving the world rather than simply trying to save souls. We need to get out and do something." Suppose that you are a member of that church, as are the activists. How would you respond to their plea, from the standpoint of pluralism in the church?

(4) Hans Küng, a widely known Roman Catholic theologian in Tübingen, Germany, has said and written some things that the Vatican finds disturbing and unacceptable. Without attempting to argue the specific merits of the case, how much dissent do you think a church ought to tolerate? If, in the name of unity, it insists on strict obedience, what happens to pluralism and progress? If, in the name of pluralism and openness, it permits any and all opinions to be expressed, what happens to its distinctiveness and authority?

# 5

# FAITH, THEOLOGY
# AND PLURALISM

The Christian faith possesses an even deeper drive toward universal oneness than does theological reflection. There is a point beyond which theological reflection, theological discussion, and theological polemic can never take us. It cannot take us to the experience of unity in the faithful Christian heart. "You can lead a horse to water, but you cannot make him drink," says the old proverb. Just so, you can lead individual persons right up to a confrontation with a new idea, but there is no way by which you can force them to embrace that new idea as their own. You can point to other persons, and you can argue vehemently that they are brothers and sisters in Christ. And nothing, except your own blood pressure, will change.

But if persons have the experience of meeting brothers and sisters across boundaries that previously seemed unbridgeable, then nothing can persuade them that it did not happen. They *know* it happened, because it happened to them!

## Antioch and Jerusalem

The Bible is a vast reservoir of human experience. Almost every sort of experience that can happen to a human being in a single lifetime happens in the pages of the Bible. More than once, as likely as not. And it is to the Bible that we turn to see, in stories of actual living, the discovery that there is more than one way to reach the gate of heaven.

The scene is Antioch, a city about 300 miles north of Jerusalem, and within easy reach of the Mediterranean coast. The time is about A.D. 40, give or take a year or two one way or the other. We are about to witness one of the most significant events in the life of the Christian church.

This is the way it came about. The stoning of Stephen had signalled the start of a determined effort by the authorities to stamp out this new religious movement—Christianity. Fearing for their lives, many of the Christians in Jerusalem had fled to Phoenicia, Cyprus and Antioch. There they quickly established themselves as useful members of the community. But these were Greek communities. And it soon became apparent that there was something different about these newcomers. They were Jews, to be sure, and they followed the Jewish religion, with which their new neighbors were familiar. But it was the Jewish religion with a difference. That difference was Jesus.

Before long, a number of Greeks were attracted to this new religion. They attended its meetings, they listened to its teachings, they became devoted followers. The Christian community in Antioch grew and prospered. In fact, here the name "Christians" was first used to describe the followers of Christ. And because the myriad Jewish dietary laws seemed to them to have nothing to do with being a Christian, the Antioch Christians gradually ceased to follow them. To this community came Paul and Barnabas, and here they stayed for a year, preaching and teaching in a house near the Pantheon.

But trouble was not far away. Back in Jerusalem were many Christians who had stayed on in spite of the persecution. They held fast to the old ways, and they insisted that to be a true follower of Jesus, one must first keep all the Jewish dietary laws. Had Jesus himself not said that it was no part of his purpose to destroy the law? Paul said that this was nonsense, that anyone could plainly see that these non-Jewish Christians were truly Christians. The fruits of the Holy Spirit were evident in their lives as surely as in the lives of the Jewish Christians.

At last, the disagreement grew so intense that a Council was called in Jerusalem. James, the brother of Jesus, was the chairperson. Paul attended to defend the interests of his Gentile Christians, taking with him a handsome gift from the church in Antioch for the relief of those who had remained faithful during the persecution. At this Council, Peter was the real hero. He defended the Gentile Christians. You must remember, he said, that we ourselves discovered we could not find peace with God through the Jewish Law. It is by grace that we who are Jews are saved. This is what Jesus has taught us. If the Law could not help us, who are Jews, why should we expect it will be of help to those who have been reared in an entirely different tradition?

86

This was the argument that won the day. James declared it made sense to him, and the whole Council agreed. According to the new ruling, the necessary dietary restrictions were minimal: all Christians should abstain from meats offered to idols, from blood, from things strangled. And Christians should abstain from fornication. If the Christians in Antioch could agree to these things, then they were all Christians together. Paul was delighted. His Gentile Christians were not about to do these things anyway. He persuaded Peter to promise he would come to Antioch shortly to visit the Gentile congregation there, and he went off toward home with a light heart.

Peter's visit to Antioch began in great style. The Antiochan Christians were obviously impressed by the rugged faith and warm personality of the big fisherman from Galilee. Peter was visibly impressed by the obvious sincerity and devotion of the Antiochan Christians. They were as one big, happy family. At their common meal following Holy Communion on Sunday night, Peter ate with them. And no one even asked whether the dietary laws had been followed in the preparation of the food.

But disaster was just around the corner. When visitors from Jerusalem arrived, Peter did an about-face. He withdrew from the fellowship when mealtime came, lest word be carried back to Jerusalem that he had failed to observe the old dietary laws. With this, many of the Jewish Christians in the church at Antioch also withdrew from the common meal. Even so staunch an ally as Barnabas joined in the withdrawal. The Gentile Christians were dismayed. So they really were second-class Christians, after all! When the pinch came, they were not good enough to have fellowship with one of the apostles. At first one, and then another, dropped by the wayside, sadly concluding that Jesus Christ was really not for them!

Paul was outraged. The work to which he had given his life was disintegrating before his eyes. He knew from personal experience that keeping the Jewish Law could never give a person the peace of Christ. He knew from personal experience that his understanding of the Christian faith was authentic. Christ himself had appeared to him on the Damascus road, and the peace of Christ had been his ever since. There was no room for compromise now. If he did not confront this issue head-on, the whole cause of Gentile Christianity was lost. Paul described his encounter with the dissembling Peter like this: "I withstood him to the face, because he was to be blamed."

We do not know in detail all that happened in Antioch, but the outcome is clear. Paul won the unquestionable right to carry Christianity to those who were not Jews, without requiring them first to become followers of the Jewish Law. Barely 20 years after Jesus had lived and taught and died, the Risen Christ had already shown the power to leap across barriers of culture and religion and class, and to win a response in the hearts and minds of men and women of an entirely different style of life.

The problem Paul confronted has a familiar sound. We need to remind ourselves—as we face a similar situation—that at the very heart of the Christian faith lies a power that has been able to deal with this kind of thing more than once in the past. We may dare to believe that this power is still at work in the world today. We just need to learn to get out of the way—travel light—and let the power of the Risen Christ do the work it has done so many times before.

## Old Testament Roots

This experience in Antioch, which set the new religion free of its ethnic, national and geographic ties and enabled it to speak to all persons everywhere, has roots deep in the Old Testament. It is common enough in the history of religions to find a priest speaking to a people on behalf of their god, assuring them that the divinity looks upon them with favor, promising them success in war, abundant crops and fertile cattle. There are even echoes of this kind of religion in the Old Testament itself. But more than once in the Old Testament, we find the prophet speaking on behalf of God *against* the people, with the clear message that God is displeased with the ways in which they have been conducting themselves. They have neglected his worship, oppressed the poor, enslaved the stranger within their gates.

Even the great King David was not exempt from the judgment of God. His adulterous affair with Bathsheba while her husband was off to war had resulted in her pregnancy, and there was no way to cover up what they had done. In desperation, David had called her husband home from the battlefield on a flimsy pretext, expecting him to seize the opportunity to spend the night at home in a comfortable bed with his beautiful wife. But Uriah, remaining stubbornly true to his soldier's vow, had refused to indulge himself. Instead, loyal soldier that he was, he had slept at the palace door with the rest of the king's servants.

His fidelity did him in! Now David had no way to avoid acknowledging the true paternity of Bathsheba's as yet unborn child. So he
sent the luckless Uriah back to the battle, having given secret instruc-
tions that he should be stationed in a position of the greatest danger,
where he would surely be killed. When the sad news came that
Bathsheba was now a widow, David was free to marry her himself.
So did the king manipulate the lives of his subjects to suit his own
whim.

In any other country in that ancient world, the story might have
ended right there. But this was Israel, and the Lord of Israel was
displeased with what David had done. He sent the prophet Nathan to
confront the king.

Nathan approached his task with consummate skill. He told David
a story about a wealthy man who was too stingy to take a lamb from
his own herd to provide a feast for an unexpected visitor but instead
stole from a poor neighbor the one ewe lamb he possessed, and
slaughtered it, even though the poor man's children had raised it as a
pet. This was an issue David could understand. He was outraged to
think anyone should be so unjust. Indignantly, he demanded to know
who this wicked man might be, so that he might be punished. And, in
words that have thundered and echoed down the corridors of time
ever since, Nathan replied bluntly, "You are the man."

It was a brave deed, for kings were absolute monarchs in those
days and one did not say no to them lightly. But Nathan did it in the
name of God. And in the name of God, David listened. Over the
course of history, people would need to learn that lesson again and
again, but its meaning is clear enough. Power is not its own excuse
for existing. Just because we are strong enough to do what we want to
do, we are not necessarily right. Even a king must obey the laws of
right and wrong. The arrogance of power has no place in the biblical
experience.

## From Jerusalem to Jericho

The tradition in the Bible of God's recognizing no measure of a
person's value except our common humanity came to its fullest
expression in Jesus. Perhaps nowhere in his teachings does it appear
with greater clarity and impact than in his parable of the Good
Samaritan.

There can be no doubt about it. Jesus was a masterful teacher. And like most whose classroom is the streetcorner or the hillside, Jesus had learned how to handle those who came to challenge and to mock, as well as those who came to learn.

Picture this scene. As Jesus was quietly talking with some of his friends one day, he became aware that a number of strangers had joined their circle. It almost seemed they had stopped by completely by chance. But Jesus knew the signals well. They were exchanging glances among them, and surreptitious signals. One was gradually working his way to a spot where he could claim the Master's attention. Then, when Jesus paused in his conversation, the man made his move. "Teacher," he said, as though he had only the greatest respect for what Jesus had been saying," what shall I do to inherit eternal life?"

At once, Jesus knew what was going on. The man may have looked like an ordinary passerby, but it was a scribe's question, and only one who understood the intricacies of the Jewish Law would ever have asked it in just that way. The man was out to trip him up, if he could. But Jesus knew how to answer him.

"What is written in the law?" he asked the man. "What do you read there?"

The man answered smoothly, "Thou shalt love the Lord thy God ... and thy neighbor as thyself."

"That's all there is to it," Jesus answered. "Do this, and you shall live."

The man was disconcerted. He had sought to put Jesus on the spot, but, with perfect courtesy, Jesus had sidestepped the spot very neatly. Instead, the man himself was on it! Jesus had made the question seem a needless one, easily answered by the law in which the man was supposed to be the expert. It was a sorry ending to what the man's friends had confidently expected would be a humiliating debate for the Master. Now he had to redeem himself in the eyes of his friends, as well as in the eyes of the circle into which he had intruded. He must show them all that Jesus was really not so astute as he had appeared. And so, to justify himself, he asked, "And who is my neighbor?"

It was a clever tactic. While it seemed innocent enough, it really impaled Jesus on one of the sharpest questions of the age. The Jews did not regard the Gentiles as their neighbors. The Greeks held the "barbarians" in similar contempt. The Romans reserved one brand of justice for those who could claim Roman citizenship and another brand for those who were less privileged. Now the pressure was on Jesus again, and all eyes turned back to him, to see how he would respond this time.

He responded by telling the story of the Good Samaritan. It was a classic comeback. Without accusing anyone, it managed to hit every prejudice by which his listeners lived. The man in trouble in the story was no one in particular. "A certain man" was the only identity Jesus gave him—and all the identity he needed. The situation he found himself in was one familiar to everyone within sound of the Master's voice, for the road from Jerusalem to Jericho was notorious as a place where a man's possessions and even his person were in constant danger from outlaw bands. Those who rendered no help were the official representatives of the religion which should have made them neighbors—though few of Jesus' hearers would really have expected much else from those professional religionists. But not a single one of Jesus' listeners would have chosen as a hero the man the Master singled out—a Samaritan, member of a despised group, follower of a religion they considered degenerate, a person with whom none of them would have had any dealings.

So did Jesus handle the question of who can really be a child of God and who remains a kind of stepchild. He did not argue. He did not write a learned theological treatise. He told a simple parable. But the disputatious scribe quickly recognized which man had proven a neighbor to the person who fell among the thieves. No one has ever really doubted it from that day to this.

## Ethnic Faith and the New Theology

Important and positive theological discoveries are still emerging today out of the daily religious experience to which the Bible calls us—and out of the religious experience of our ethnic minorities, as they live each day with the realities of prejudice and racism. In theological parlance, this is called "contextual theology"—a theology which avowedly thinks within the experience of a particular group. Some resist the kind of theology that develops out of the ethnic experience. What we need, they say, is a universal understanding of the faith for all people everywhere, not a theology that comes out of the partial and limited experience of any group.

Those who make such objections, however, fail to realize that all theology is contextual theology. The fact that, up to now, most theology has been the work of the dominant white minority does not mean that it has not been limited and partial. As a matter of fact, the white person thinks within the limits of white experience just as surely as the black person and the red person think within the limits of theirs.

We are impoverished theologically, as in all areas of life, by the fact that important aspects of human experience have been missing from the thinking of the dominant culture. What we need is a truly pluralistic theology, a theology that reflects the full range of human experience because it rests not on white experience alone, but on the wider experience of the human race, and includes the contributions of all ethnic groups. To this kind of theology, Benjamin Reist has given the name "pentagular theology," or five-sided theology, because it includes not only white experience, but red, yellow, black and brown experience as well.

Because of the particular history of blacks in the United States, black theology was the first to discover this need for a new theological construction and has led us into new ways of approaching our theological task. It departed from the Euro-American way of theological reflection. It moved us from a theology of "right thinking" (orthodoxy) to a theology of "right doing" (ortho-praxis). Black theological thinkers realized that ethics had outrun our theologies. What black theology said was that the church could no longer engage in what Paul Tillich called the "denial of justice in the name of holiness."

While it is a legitimate criticism that black theology was primarily preoccupied with the race problem as it related to black and white, its thinking led, nevertheless, to universal theological truths that can be helpful in theological discussion that goes far beyond race. Black theology has helped us reencounter the truth that Jesus Christ transcends all tribes, cultures, races and ethnic groups, but demands of none of them that they relinquish their identities. As Gayraud Wilmore has observed in a recent article titled "The New Context of Black Theology in the United States": "Black theology demonstrates that Jesus Christ can be de-Americanized without losing his essential meaning as the incarnate Son of God who takes away the sins of the world by his cross and resurrection."[1]

But in truth we are only beginning to learn what it will mean when ethnic minorities are given the opportunity to engage in a broadly inclusive pluralistic theological discussion. And it must become our purpose to initiate, encourage and promote that conversation among ethnic minorities in America, who can make us all more aware and more able to participate in a world context with our brothers and sisters whose faith has been shaped and nurtured by the cultural experience in Latin America, Africa, Asia and the Pacific.

Such theological reflection can help save the church and its theological institutions from a theological narcissism in which theological educators simply use a European mirror that allows them only to see themselves and to look backward. A pluralistic theological enterprise will include an ideological ingredient which will not allow present-day racism, with all of its intellectual respectability and aura of erudition, to lull theological educators into taking racism lightly. It will, in effect, attempt to "redeem the seminaries"—to use Roy Sano's phrase.[2]

Pluralistic theological reflection should not, by any means, be confined to the seminaries alone. Local church groups in every region ought to seek to engage persons of the Third World and be broadened and challenged by their cultural and theological reflections on the meaning of the Christian faith through their eyes and experience. Many of these minority persons have caught visions of God at work in this time of history and are reading the signs of the times.

Though bitter memories, ill-fated efforts and premature partnerships of the past counsel that caution and care must be taken in forging a broadly inclusive, multi-ethnic theology, the time for that conversation is clearly upon us.

The effort must not sacrifice the unique and distinctive gifts and identities which each group brings from its own historical and cultural background. To do so is to deny the richness of genuine pluralism and to make a mockery of truth and creation. On the other hand, ethnic pluralism cannot be allowed to substitute symbols for substance and consensus for the Cross of Christ. We must raise some questions for which easy and time-worn answers will not be adequate. We must probe some problems which mundane solutions will not satisfy.

Theological reflection must be reevaluated in the light of the needs of ethnic minorities and the gifts they offer the whole church. Institutions and individuals must help us eagerly receive those gifts. Native Americans can educate us in poetry of religious expression, joy in creation, reverence for all things and a passionate attachment. The Hispanic-Americans can teach us to celebrate life and not subdue it. They can provide a joy, warmth and spontaneity that supply an enriching contrast to a technological, pragmatic outlook and the formal and often arid worship of the Anglo Church. The Asian-Americans, out of their long, rich and diverse background, can help us discover the value of an emphasis on life-oriented qualities such as joy, spontaneity, intuitiveness, respect for the family and the elderly, and can contribute an amazing ability to synthesize and to bring unity from diversity. Black Americans can help us learn how to bring joy out of sorrow, to celebrate in the midst of pain, to see the sacred and secular as a unity, to affirm life and to know that blues and spirituals are but different stanzas of the same song—one on Saturday night and the other on Sunday morning.

## The Wide World of Pluralism

The call for pluralism grows louder and clearer with each day's news broadcast, and our faith and our theology must listen to the message and rise to the call. Consider some significant signs of the times: the greatly increased consciousness of women, clearly seen in the interest in the Equal Rights Amendment and other feminist issues; the influence of Third World people's assertion of their own identity, evident, for example, in the success of two recent television mini-series, *Roots* and *Shogun*, and accompanied by a general post-Freudian rise in awareness of the individual's search for identity; the considerable reduction in European colonialism; the diminished effectiveness of the American assimilation process; a revealing exegesis of American imperialism in Southeast Asia; the resumed diplomatic relationship with the People's Republic of China; the change in the implementation of immigration laws, and the increased number of independent African nations. All these changes—and there are many more—demand unprecedented shifts in our perspective on pluralism and our perceptions of ourselves in a global world that is interdependent and in a nation that is comprised of so many racial and ethnic groups.

In our shrinking globe we cannot afford cultural illiteracy. In our nation with such vast numbers of ethnic minorities we can no longer pay the price that cultural arrogance demands. In the words of Horace Kallen, "Abundance, to say nothing of completeness, is impossible without pluralism. Scarcity is impossible without monism."

The Committee on International Affairs of the Canadian Council of Churches found themselves arriving at such a position in the light of their understanding of living in an interdependent world. Their conclusion was: "Our national life cannot be deemed healthy, happy and enjoyable if it is achieved at the expense of others or if it simply accepts in perpetuity a relative gap between affluence and poverty."[3]

The Christian faith calls us to faithful obedience to Jesus Christ in whatever place. If the church is to carry out that mandate, it must reassess what that means with ethical and theological integrity. Franklin Littell's comment is probably correct: "self-analysis and self-discovery in the religious bodies may have considerable value in clarifying some cultural, social and political issues."[4] The distinction between the Christian faith and American culture must be made. Surely Christ stands *above* culture and gives the ultimate value reference for any society. Jesus Christ transcends all cultures, tribes and lands. The God who was in Christ reconciling the world to himself is not the least bit interested in the survival or extension of Western culture, but rather that we all shall see the essential meaning and live out the faith in the Incarnate Son of God who takes away the sins of the whole world by his crucifixion and resurrection.

Cultural arrogance is excess baggage and has no place on the pilgrimage of faith and works we have been contemplating. It is our cultural arrogance which has made it all but impossible for us to understand in what ways Christ may indeed be against us in this present hour. King David was a mightly ruler, but he was not too arrogant or too powerful to listen to Nathan's words. Is there something prophetic we should hear in the call to pluralism that sounds today from the strangers-at-home in our local and our global community?

# CHAPTER 5: RECALL/RESPONSE

## RECALL

"The Christian faith calls us to faithful obedience to Jesus Christ in whatever place. If the church is to carry out that mandate, it must reassess what that means with ethical and theological integrity. . . . Surely Christ stands *above* culture and gives the ultimate value reference for any society."

"The call for pluralism grows louder and clearer with each day's news broadcast, and our faith and our theology must listen to the message and rise to the call. . . . All these changes . . . demand unprecedented shifts in our perspective on pluralism and our perceptions of ourselves in a global world that is interdependent and in a nation comprised of so many racial and ethnic groups."

"The problem Paul confronted [at Antioch] has a familiar sound. We need to remind ourselves—as we face a similar situation—that at the very heart of the Christian faith lies a power that has been able to deal with this kind of thing more than once in the past. We may dare to believe that this power is still at work in the world today."

## RESPONSE

(1) Has your contact with persons of other ethnic and/or racial groups affected your concept of God? How? Is this reflected in the church you attend? In what ways? If not, how would you personally like to see it reflected?

(2) Your church is located in a community in which only one racial and ethnic group lives. In a discussion in the women's group, a newcomer states that she feels that her children are being deprived of a "realistic view of the world," since they do not come in contact with people who are different racially, culturally and ethnically. What alternatives can be offered to this mother? What steps might be taken to allay her concern, short of suggesting she find another church or community?

(3) Design a comprehensive (12-week) intercultural educational program for your local church that will include action experiences for the participants. These can be done in small groups and shared with the class. Such a program may include a plan to take a trip to another

country (non-Western) and the preparation for experiencing that culture in a nonjudgmental way in order to learn from that culture. Design your program to encourage awareness of the ways we are prisoners of our own culture.

(4) Plan a multi-cultural event in which the major ethnic minorities' histories in North America will be reconstructed. Arts, foods, festivals, rituals, music, poetry and other elements may be used.

Experiences to help groups determine what assumptions, biases, attitudes, beliefs and values have shaped their lives should be provided. Thus, the following should be examined: (a) the concept of America as a "chosen people," (b) individualism versus communal responsibilities, (c) the gospel of wealth and success, (d) concepts of time, work and space, (e) private ownership versus communal ownership, (f) competitiveness, aggression, self-indulgence and other American characteristics that may not be evident in other cultures.

(5) Robert Bellah says in *The Broken Covenant:* "We need to learn how to wait as well as to act. We do not know what the future holds and we must give up the illusion that we can control it for we know it depends not only on our action but on grace." Do you agree? If so, restate this in terms of a specific event or case in your local church. If you do not agree, refute this in terms of a specific example in your local church.

(6) Take a daily newspaper and go through it, clipping articles that promote pluralism and others that impede pluralism. Explain why you chose these.

# 6

## PLURALISM IN CONTEXT

Several leading thinkers in America over the last century, such as William James, Randolph Bourne, Isaac Berkson and Horace Kallen, have offered original conceptions and a variety of proposals for pluralism.[1] Perhaps the classical study was done by Kallen, who devoted a great deal of his life and work to the development and promotion of the concept. His clearest statement was made in two lectures given at the Greenfield Center for Human Relations at the University of Pennsylvania in 1954 and was expanded into a volume entitled *Cultural Pluralism and the American Idea*. Here he sets forth his basic idea:

> A living culture is a changing culture; and it is a changing culture, and not an auctioneer's storage house or an archaeologist's dump of fragments, fossils and ruins, because of the transactions wherewith living, altering individuals transform old thoughts and things while laboring to preserve them and to produce new. Cultures live and grow in and through the individual, and their vitality is a function of individual diversities of interests and associations. Pluralism is the *sine qua non* of their persistence and prosperous growth. But not the absolutist pluralism which the concept of the unaltering and inalterable Monad discloses. On the contrary, the *sine qua non* is fluid, relational pluralism which the living individual encounters in the transactions wherewith he [sic] constructs his personal history moving out of groups and into groups, engaging in open or hidden communion with societies of his fellows, every one different from the others, and all teamed together, and struggling to provide and maintain the common means which nourish, assure, enhance, the different, and often competing, values they differently cherish.[2]

## Pluralism as Fulfillment and as Problem

Critical of the effort by the dominant "nativism" of Anglo-Saxon Protestants to create a mono-culture, Kallen argues that cultural pluralism is the fulfillment of "the American Idea." He postulates that this process is "an orchestration of diverse utterances of diversities" involving regional, local, religious, ethnic, esthetic, political and recreational—developing freely and characteristically in its own enclave, and so intertwined with the others as to suggest and even to symbolize the dynamic of the whole. Each of these "cultural reservoirs" flows into its own singularity of expression to unite in "the concrete intercultural total which is the culture of America." He clearly points out the "inter-cultural" nature of the enterprise, to avoid segregation and isolation, and the parity of each as both cooperators and competitors.

Kallen interprets the third of the "inalienable rights" which the Declaration of Independence guarantees, "the pursuit of happiness," as meaning "the cultivation of life, guided by faith and worked out by patterned conduct, the two together creating an individual biography or a communal history, the linkage of whose events is a practical orchestration of an imaginative vision of nature, man, and man's destiny."[3] Thus, the "pursuit of happiness" for him is that cultures and their diversities be peers and equals, and endeavor to preserve, enrich and perfect themselves through *free* exchange of thoughts and things with all humankind. Such a cultural pluralism allows for the least amount of injustice, frustration or suppression of any culture (local, national or international) by the other.

Cultural pluralism raises a number of issues that must be faced. Kallen realized that and began a talk on pluralism at Howard University, a predominantly black school in Washington, in 1955 by saying: "Cultural pluralism is a controversial expression. It has been such from the day it first figured in the public prints."[4] While a number of factors have changed since that lecture was given, as we have already noted, and while pluralism is a more popular notion today, there are real dilemmas that pluralism raises.

Before we look at these dilemmas, a few clarifications are in order. First, it must be said quite clearly that while we have documented the decline of the Anglo-American Protestant leadership and the American ideal of the assimilation process and the myth of the melting pot, citing a number of studies, it must not be assumed that the crisis we face in culture, the present cultural depravity, the loss of national ideals and the current anomie in American institutions can be assigned solely to the failure of Protestantism. The assimilation process *did* work in the past and continues, to some extent, and many white ethnic groups were assimilated into American culture and became clearly identified with the prevailing culture and the values, ideals, behaviors and other components of the culture and enjoyed the benefits therefrom. Orlando Patterson, in an article in *The American Scholar* entitled "On Guilt, Relativism and Black-White Relations,"[5] points out that we must distinguish among three concepts: the *idea* of the melting pot, which is a "cosmopolitan ideal"; the *myth* of the melting pot, which is the social fiction that the ideal had been realized when, in fact, the reality was far from it; and the *reality* of the melting pot, which is the actual extent to which the melting pot ideal had been accomplished, independent of exaggerations and myths about it.

Second, while there were and are many contradictions in values that have not been resolved, these have operated, to some extent, as bipolarities of a whole in a kind of dialectic: between open and closed, inclusive and exclusive, cosmopolitan and local, egalitarian and authoritarian, melting pot and Anglo-conformist, cooperative and competitive, internationalist and isolationist.

Third, the nation's overreliance on science and technology to solve human problems has proven to be a serious mistake. While they can produce, and have produced, much to make life more humane and comfortable, science and technology without some serious commitment to human ends and a qualitative faith in the equitable distribution of resources among human persons can prove to be a real menace—a frightening reality with which our present society is faced.

## Dilemmas of Pluralism

While a discussion of pluralism does not raise quite as many eyebrows and tempers today as it once did, the notion is by no means instantly accepted by all. A writer in the *Journal of Politics* in 1977 referred to "the conservatism of pluralists in politics (and research)." Orlando Patterson's recent book, *Ethnic Chauvinism: The Reactionary Impulse* argues against pluralism. Stein and Hill in *The Ethnic Imperative* warn that if pluralism is embraced as the wave of

101

the future, we are "building the future from our fears, rather than our hopes and aspirations." *The International Encyclopedia of Social Science* says matter-of-factly, "The pluralist position . . . may be viewed as a conservative reaction against the presumed effects of a main society."

Yet the fact of pluralism persists because diversity is present. As with dandelions in the grass, so with differences: as soon as you think you are rid of them, new ones appear somewhere else on the lawn. Our present blue jeans craze illustrates the point. While jeans were supposed to put an end to the distinctions in dress, new and different ones keep appearing, by ever more creative designers, so that now connoisseurs of blue jeans can recognize a thousand new distinctions.

The concept of pluralism does raise a number of dilemmas. Though maintaining that there is a bankruptcy in prevailing values, a depravity in culture, we cannot then simply assume that an unexamined and unqualified pluralism is the panacea for intergroup relations in American society. Let us look at some of the dilemmas raised by pluralism in an effort to reappraise some of the assumptions about it.

### The Dilemma of Relativism

Some charge that pluralism depends on relativism, that relativism necessarily regresses to primitivism and barbarism, and that because of this tendency, pluralism could destroy the progress made in equality of opportunity. The charge that pluralism is a statement of relativism is relatively true. It cannot be denied that pluralism rests on the assumption that each culture must be treated on its own terms because of the basic premise that the values, attitudes, sentiments and ideas of each group are determined by that group's own peculiar and specific cultural tradition.

A few basic risks can be identified if relativism is made an absolute. These have been cited by Orlando Patterson in the article quoted earlier and by Howard F. Stein and Robert F. Hill in a recent book, *The Ethnic Imperative*. A brief summary of some of their objections can be stated.

1. It runs the risk of being self-contradictory. It asserts a general value (the values of all peoples are of equal worth), then contradicts it by implying the superiority of the position of the relativists (other peoples must be seen in their own terms), a value not necessarily held by persons who do not share the relativist point of view.

102

2. Relativism, while aimed at an ideal of tolerance, can be associated with a reactionary view of the world and can be used to rationalize inaction, complacency and even gross forms of oppression. It is all too easy, for example, for the white South African, or American, to say that it is wrong to interfere with the way of life of the reservation Bantus or Native Americans, since "what might appear to be squalor and backwardness to us, may be matters of great virtue to them."[6]

3. It is nonreciprocal and, as such, easily degenerates into unintended patronage. In relating to minorities, the white pluralist is trapped in a patronizing situation, for to "relate relativistically" implies that cultural and moral differences exist but that one is refusing to accept the existence of such differences. To the astonishment of the white pluralist, he will find that "he has exposed himself to the charges of double standards, or moral superiority, or both."[7]

While these dangers must be considered by those who would take pluralism seriously, the dilemma of relativism is somewhat exaggerated. It is spoken of as if there were no other factors in the American context to regulate intergroup relations. The pervasiveness of industrialism, technology, and the mass media are not considered. Also, the Constitution sets forth some basic laws that guarantee and regulate individual rights that are not affected by relativism. And a number of bills have been passed and court rulings handed down in the last two decades that are precisely aimed at regulatory measures in civil rights. But most important is the fact that most people are *within* the culture and not *outside* of it and therefore will clearly work to share in many of the benefits it has to offer. Could it be intellectual snobbishness or condescension to suggest that ethnic and cultural minorities are not capable of judging and deciding when actions infringe upon or decrease such equality of opportunity as has already been gained in the society? Surely ethnic minorities and cultural groups can develop alternate understandings of what success means and chart what trade-offs are involved.

### The Dilemma of Factionalism

Second, it is charged that pluralism leads to fragmented, hostile factions. Decrying the "New Ethnicity" as "a static and vigilantly defended closed system," some observers insist that pluralism "destroys the individual by offering him or her the freedom of a one-dimensional identity." When persons are treated as a corporate entity and representatives of a taxonomic class, demands for group rights, "Affirmative Action," "quotas" and the hiring of personnel on the basis of ascriptive criteria are an extension. The fear is expressed by the sociologists Stein and Hill: "It is probably only a matter of time until every self-defined and politically powerful *minority* is able to apply pressure from its lobby for a reparative and remedial quota, thereby making the American mosaic a collectivity of fragmented islands united only by the sea of discontent and animosity."[8]

Further, it is charged, "Affirmative action and similar pluralist affirmations lock the individual (while rewarding him or her) into the very straitjacket he or she may want to escape."[9] Arguing that there can be no individual justice where group or corporate justice prevails, these observers of society insist: "One is rewarded not for competence, but for being black, Polish, or female, not for being an individual but representing the group."[10]

In the first place, both the Stein and Hill volume and Orlando Patterson's writings confuse cultural pluralism with ethnicity. The pluralism that has been proposed by most recent scholars and certainly is proposed in this book is a concern for a cultivation of *respect* for the background and identity of culturally distinct people, and an avoidance of domination by white Anglo-Saxon culture, not the perpetuation of cultures with conflicting values at any cost. This pluralism does not negate a common core of central values. It does not encourage or promote a massive withdrawal from universalistic ideals, with a new kind of fascism where each ethnic group becomes totally ethnocentric and regards its own values as superior to universal values. In fact, this pluralism seriously questions whether the Anglo-Saxon Protestant values as actualized in America and adopted by white ethnic groups were universal enough. It faults the process of assimilation, with its inability to include all ethnic groups, for failure to achieve one universal human family, a family with many members differing from one another in color, beliefs, and culture and yet respected and affirmed as full participating members of the human family.

Patterson argues for the universalism of "pristine Christianity" (which he defines as "religion which had been that of Jesus"), in contrast to the particularism that issues from one-dimensional identity.[11] But he does not face the fact that there was a central conflict in pristine Christianity over the right of the Gentiles to express the faith and life of Jesus in their own cultural style. The historic confrontation between Peter and Paul at Antioch concerned this very question.[12] The decision was that the Gentiles would not be required to adopt Hebrew ways in order to be Christian. This was most certainly a decision in favor of cultural pluralism.

The charge that pluralism leads to Affirmative Action and thus locks individuals into "straitjackets" they may want to escape, must be addressed. The arguments about Affirmative Action have been long and heated. The controversy continues. Stein and Hill join the many who contend that Affirmative Action amounts to an official policy of reverse discrimination (discrimination against majority members of society) or preferential treatment on the basis of sex or race. Their contention is that its pluralist affirmation robs the person of his or her individuality for the sake of the person's group identity.

There is not space, nor is it the intent of this book, to make the case for or against Affirmative Action. That can better be done elsewhere and has been.[13]. However, a word about the subject is in order. Clearly, in Affirmative Action the normative principles are equality, distributive justice and compensatory justice—not a matter of individualism versus corporatism, to which it is reduced by the argument presented above. The traditional view that identifiable skills, competencies or abilities alone are relevant to admissions or employment must be challenged on several grounds: (1) The use of the performance of white, middle-class males as our standard of excellence continues a cultural bias unreflective of the diversity of the society. (2) Traditional criteria for success in schools, business and other areas may not be entirely accurate. Role models may be a relevant part of the criteria. (3) Minority groups are appropriate recipients of the good offered by Affirmative Action, because of the past and present wrongs they have suffered. (4) Even when traditional qualifications are changed, the assumption that qualification is the sole or most appropriate test for deserving employment or admission must be questioned.

To elaborate on the fourth point, we cannot assume that the "best qualified person" is necessarily the one who deserves the position. The needs of and advantages to minority persons are other criteria for deserving. The possession of specific abilities or disabilities is very often not determined by the individual, but by socio-economic, environmental and cultural factors, physiological characteristics (e.g., sex) and other determiners. These determiners cannot be said to be deserved or undeserved, and should not have the power to determine deservingness of employment or admission.

Dr. Richard Wasserstrom of the University of California argues that in a university setting, the presence of minority persons (faculty and students) is instrumentally related to the fulfillment of an essential function of the university—the quest for truth. Race and sex, according to him, are such central features of our experience that they determine in basic ways the manner in which persons perceive and respond to the world.

> If race and sex have a significant effect upon the evolution of entire academic disciplines—the way in which problems are formulated and defined in those disciplines—and consequently on what comes to be believed and labeled knowledge, then the addition of minority persons to the student body and faculty will increase the probability that important truths will be discovered, for minority persons and women would conceive of problems and issues in new and different perspectives, furthering the quest for truth and knowledge.[14]

The appointment/hiring/admissions of women and minorities to comply with Affirmative Action directives, regarded by some as "straitjacketing" those persons into the very categories they are trying to overcome and making them "tokens," is simultaneously positive and negative. These minority members might not choose the quota system or Affirmative Action route to force the issue of their own advancement, but without such a route the "white male club" would, as it always has, deny them equitable access to positions of power where they are able to prove themselves "deserving" through their own skills and qualifications. Affirmative Action is simply an example of a less-than-perfect means justifying an equitable, just, and necessary end. Affirmative Action, in and of itself, does not push one up the corporate ladder or through educational rounds but simply opens the door; it does not "reward" a minority individual or group for their minority status or even make reparation and restitution for past injustices but simply removes roadblocks to the starting gate.

*The Dilemma of Resegregation*

Another dilemma is the charge that pluralism leads to separatism or resegregation. This has been referred to variously as "refeudalization," "Balkanization," the "Southern model" and so on.

In good conscience and in the best interest of all, let us hope the sordid history of segregation in America, with its costly effects, is over. The Civil Rights Movement, the marches, fire hoses, dogs, cattle prods, the burning and bombing of churches and the immense ultimate payment in life itself by so many led to the passage of the civil rights legislation to end public segregation—hopefully forever. Ethnic pluralism does not call for segregation, but it recognizes that integration predicated on the notion that all must become the same and fit into white-dominated institutions and become mere copies of Anglo-Saxon Americans denies the greatest possibility of fulfillment the pluralism offers—a recognition and an appreciation of diversities and the gifts they offer for the greater whole.

What black people insist on is not merely to be seen as white people with black skin, as black Anglo-Saxon Americans. Color blindness in vision is seen as a pathology to be corrected, not a condition to aspire to. And pluralism goes far beyond the slogan "Black is beautiful!" It is sometimes and sometimes it is not. Pluralism calls for a sensitivity to the reality of ethnic groups and a celebration of the ethnic variety of America. Pluralism does not mean segregation into groups by color; it also does not mean that if a whole group happens to be black, brown, yellow or red, it is therefore to be condemned and judged inferior for lack of white presence to give it legitimacy.

Understandably, there is concern about segregation and separatism. These would certainly be steps in the wrong direction. But, just as certainly, integrated powerlessness and an integration that requires persons to deny differences and simply to affirm the validity of white traditions and white values is neither plausible nor desirable. What pluralism asserts is something beyond integration—the ability to be at home with all persons. This is the other-side-of-the-coin of the old truth that people must be at home somewhere before they can create a home anywhere.

There is the danger that white ethnic groups may use ethnic consciousness as a ploy for racial exclusion. But that danger is present also without pluralism. It means that the new consciousness is not complete. It is worth the risk to believe that Michael Novak is right: "In possessing our own particularity we come to feel at home with ourselves and are best able to enter communion with others, freely giving and receiving of each other. . . . The point of becoming

107

ethnically alert and self-possessed is not self-enclosure; it is genuine community, honest and unpretending."[15]

A new consciousness will help persons to develop an entirely new perspective on themselves, their own culture and background, and a new perspective on other people and the world. Pluralism is a part of that new lifestyle, along with openness, acceptance of feelings of appreciation and the beauty of oneself and of others, honesty and willingness to enter into community. In a real sense it is liberation from an old way of life which ghettoized, entrapped and enslaved. It is the freedom to recognize and celebrate the multi-cultural and multi-ethnic and multi-racial character of our country and our world.

The caution which must be taken very seriously is that our children do not become so imprisoned by strong sub-cultural identities and loyalties that they do not receive the benefits that are present in the super-culture and miss the contributions that both can make to their development as citizens of both cultures. Ethnic minorities have had much more experience in this area than white groups. Perhaps a page from their book will prove helpful in avoiding this pitfall, as it has in a number of other areas. It is a blessing in disguise that black people, for instance, learn early in life what W.E.B. DuBois recognized as his "twoness." Hispanic- and Asian-Americans and, to a lesser extent, most Native Americans have also learned well how to be bi-cultural in America—sometimes out of the necessity to survive. But with genuine pluralism operative, it becomes a conscious, legitimate and even celebrated choice.

## Why Pluralism Should Be Taken Seriously

A number of factors provide compelling reasons why pluralism should be taken seriously. Some of those have been touched on in our previous discussion. Let us be a bit more specific and list them.

1. *Pluralism should be taken seriously because it provides a source of creative competition among different systems of beliefs and values which can provide a hedge against totalitarian suppression of civil rights and the establishment of a mono-culture.*

Extensive studies have shown that a multiplication of loyalties rather than the suppression of them broadens persons' conception of the world and increases their understanding of universalization. It is common to refer to persons who have had wide experience in other cultures, who have travelled to other lands and who speak several languages, as "very cultured" or "broadminded."

Is it not a contradiction, and revealing of our own sociology and cultural racism, that we developed the strange description "culturally deprived" to refer to poor and disadvantaged ethnic groups in this country or persons overseas who live in primitive settings amidst poverty and are unaffected by modernization? What the term came to connote, and probably still does to the white majority, is black, Puerto Rican, Haitian and Cuban neighborhoods, with the assumption that if persons do not hear European symphonies and attend white plays, they are deprived of "culture." A judgment had obviously been made that "culture" refers to European-oriented aspects of the arts. John Hightower of the Museum of Modern Art in New York City pointed out, however, in a 1970 issue of *Saturday Review,* that these so-called ghettos are re-teaching the real meaning of the arts: "that the arts are about people—the way they move, the things they see, the sounds they make. It may be that the ghettos will teach us once again how to sing about ourselves in a way that reminds us that the beauty and quality of all our lives and the content of our arts [are] inseparable."

What we are beginning to discover is that culturally illiterate persons—or, to use the common phrase, "culturally deprived" persons—are all persons who have no knowledge, experience or meaningful encounter with persons of another lifestyle or culture. Exposure to persons with different values, lifestyles, attitudes and histories challenges our presuppositions and prejudices and forces us to rethink our own attitudes, beliefs, values and lifestyles. We can grow through meaningful encounter and dialogue with persons and groups who will not simply reinforce our prejudices, but will challenge our assumptions. When members of a majority cultural group are locked into their own cultural existence, they suffer, for they are deprived of many rich values that may come to them from authentic interaction with other cultural groupings. Often Americans are surprised that these persons speak more than one language, whereas most Americans are single-language persons.

Pluralism encourages bi-cultural and multi-cultural identities. Encouragement of this development will give us not only a renewed respect for our own country with its many cultural and ethnic groups, but also an appreciation of true universalism, in which the merits and the weaknesses of other belief systems can be more appropriately assessed because persons or groups deeply understand and appreciate more than one culture.

In the United States the many ethnic and cultural groups provide a good beginning for that process. We have the opportunity through self-discovery and the discovery of others, to transcend the barriers that separate people from one another; to break the chains that bind people to a dead past, a "Broken Covenant," in Bellah's words, and face a future alive with the possibilities of true pluralism. We have many resources to put up a hedge against any encroaching homebred totalitarian hostility toward America's realizing its "democratic cultural pluralism," which Harold Cruse so caustically described in our earlier discussion as "the product of a badly-bungled process of inter-group cultural fusion."

2. *Pluralism should be taken seriously because it can reduce great inequities in the distribution of respect and self-respect among people.*

We noted earlier that the Anglo-American culture faces a serious crisis in moral leadership. E. Digsby Baltzell assigned the decline and failure to the Protestant Establishment's inability or unwillingness to incorporate "talented and distinguished members of minority groups into its privileged ranks." Perhaps part of that inability or unwillingness was based on the dominant culture's persistence in denying the validity of other cultural values, norms and lifestyles. In short, there was a genuine lack of respect for differences.

This is not simply a hollow cliché. It is a persistent reality. It is not uncommon in our present day to overhear American tourists in countries where there are real differences in culture and customs, remark, "They are no different than the folks back home—they are just like us." *Are* they "just like us"? In most such cases there has not been enough contact with the people and the culture, enough systematic study and intercourse with the culture, to make that determination. Usually these travellers are simply viewing another culture and people through their own eyes (culturally conditioned and single-context) and drawing conclusions. But that is not the main point; why do they *have* to be "just like us"? Inequity in respect and appreciation for other cultures leads to inequities in the respect for the persons of that culture.

Just as "all men are created equal" does not mean equal in

110

intelligence, abilities, skills, knowledge or talent, but deserving of respect, so all cultures are not equal in all components and in their ability to achieve specific universal ideals, but they deserve to be respected and understood and seen as able to contribute to a greater whole, and even expected to contribute. But in a society where considerable weight is placed on conformity to a dominant mold and one culture is weighted over another, there is no chance to choose those aspects of each that can be useful to a whole. In our society, color, ethnicity, religious practices, customs, languages, food and other aspects of cultures different from the Anglo-Saxon Protestant culture have been viewed in a negative light for a long time and therefore not respected. They were systematically turned into crushing negatives by the dominant culture. Through this negativism and unnatural isolation—a carefully monitored sifting process—the values, language, art, music, and other such elements of minority culture were not allowed substantially to influence "American" culture. It developed without contest to favor what was white and Western.

If different cultures are allowed to come into contact with one another, a new culture will be created from the strongest and best elements of each. While there may be, and most probably will be, cultural conflict, as history demonstrated when the Greek and Roman cultures collided, the result will be the birth of a new, enriched culture in which the most cogent aspects of each appear.

Pluralism can prevent the contacts among cultures from being violent ones. Characterized by openness, free access and mutual respect, pluralism allows persons and groups to discover the incredible richness and variety of other cultures and lifestyles and to borrow from one another as good neighbors always do. And it is a reciprocal process. It does not destroy the goodness and beauty of one culture to supplant it with that of another. Rather, it affirms that unity and diversity go together as partners in pluralism rather than as enemies in mono-culturalism.

Some of this has begun to happen in America as groups have rediscovered their identity and roots and more boldly insist on respect for their traditions' identities and background. Pluralism discourages inequities in respect for cultures and peoples and fosters self-respect. What it calls for is not simply romanticized notions of exotic foods and naive exclamations of one's enchantment with different customs,

111

but something far stronger: a genuine respect for other members of the human family and opportunities to break down the walls that separate people, to destroy false stereotypes and prejudices and to discover the interdependence of the human community.

3. *Pluralism should be taken seriously because it promotes a global understanding and encourages self-determination and interdependence.*

It is a strange phenomenon that we refer to "colored" people in America as "minorities" when 70 percent of the world's population is "colored." On a worldwide scale, white people are a minority. But their influence, power, affluence and control are far out of proportion to their numbers.

America became, during the early part of this century, amazingly preoccupied with success in business. The image of a broken and defeated Woodrow Wilson sitting in the White House in virtual seclusion after he failed to win the congressional support needed for the League of Nations is one of the strange ironies of this century. His reputed comment to a young Franklin Delano Roosevelt was prophetic of things to come: "It is only once in a generation that a people can be lifted above material things."[16]

Symbolizing that era and capturing its mood, Bruce Barton, an advertising executive, wrote a best-seller, *The Man Nobody Knew: A Discovery of the Real Jesus*, in which he pictured Jesus as "the most popular dinner guest in Jerusalem," a great executive who "picked up twelve men from the bottom ranks of business and forged them into an organization that conquered the world." In an era basking in success and worshipping salesmanship there was a natural receptiveness to Barton's clever theme that "the parables were the most powerful advertisement of all time" and that Jesus Christ was "the founder of modern business" and would surely have been a "national advertiser today."

Although the era ended in the stock market crash of 1929 and a policy of isolationism, it was but a short step to World War II and America's assumption of global leadership and global intervention and security management of the "free world." The effort to contain international Communism and the embarkment on a vast military aid program have led to a system of militarism whose consequences pose great problems for the world today.

With the change in foreign policy also came new political and economic policies. The growth of huge multinational corporations poses tremendous problems for peace and understanding between the industrialized countries of the West and the developing nations of the Third World. The decade of the 60's was the "first development decade," and was characterized by the residual colonialist belief that the dominant group had the means and know-how of development. The "underdeveloped" had only to follow. This attitude translated into the Western churches as the mistaken notion that it was our prerogative to be "in mission" while others were the "objects" of our mission activity. "Unlimited growth" and availability of resources were taken for granted.

This period came to an end in the late 60's. The decade of the 70's was marked by an awareness that the "underdevelopment" of some portions of the globe is inextricably related to the "overdevelopment" of other portions. As this awareness dawned on suppressed and oppressed groups in this country and abroad, earlier on some than on others, it produced radical shifts in consciousness and led to new strategies of moratorium and disengagement. There were also strategies of empowerment signalling an intention to share power, to redistribute resources and to enable a more pluralistic world and church.

Now we find ourselves, in the 80's, faced with the challenge of discovering the meaning of an inclusive church in a pluralistic society, amid the becalming winds of reaction. Clearly, pluralism requires self-determination and self-reliance within a global people who are interdependent. The missionary enterprise of the church is not a venture in scarcely disguised arrogance; it is a dialogical venture of discovery—a giving and receiving. It is a partnership in pluralism.

4. *Pluralism should be considered seriously because for many it is an already ineradicable reality.*

Many persons of ethnic minority groups live with the constant reality that they are hyphenated Americans. It was this "twoness" that W.E.B. Dubois recognized and struggled with virtually all of his long and productive life—being black and being an American. His classic work, *The Souls of Black Folks,* is a passionate and anguished poetic documentation of the struggle of the souls of black people in America. Millions of Asian- and Hispanic-Americans commute be-

113

tween two cultures—at home to varying degrees in both. Problems arise because the dominant culture places a higher value on one and a lower value on the other.

An Asian woman in San Francisco expressed the feeling and the experience of many ethnic minorities: "As a person of both cultures, I have seen values in both. The respect for the aged, the relationships that are present in the family in Asian culture, I should like to see preserved."

Roy I. Sano, Professor of Asian American Studies at the Pacific School of Religion in Berkeley, California, has offered a useful description and analysis of this process. Instead of choosing either the Euro-American cultural tradition or the cultural heritage of their own people, ethnic minority groups are working with both. "We are not simply living in social structures of the dominant society, or in our ethnic communities alone, but both. In that sense we are 'socially amphibious' along with being bi-cultural."[17] Sano believes that three distinct processes are taking place at the same time: acculturation continues; second, riches of ancestral heritages are being recovered; and third, new cultures are produced from the combination. Thus, "we have acculturation, cultural retrieval and cultural creativity."[18] Sano refers to ethnics as "socially amphibious," i.e., spending time in organizations and institutions that are primarily white while recovering ties with ethnic communities, which nurture their ethnic members. He commends this process and turns his observation into a prescription: it is the desirable route to go. This is clearly a model of pluralism that is a reality for many ethnic minority persons. It must be taken seriously. It has implications for all.

5. *Pluralism must be taken seriously because it makes us take identity seriously.*

The comment of Mahatma Gandhi is descriptive of pluralism: "I want the winds of all cultures to blow freely about my house, but not to be swept off my feet by any." Pluralism encourages self-discovery and self-knowledge, an appreciation for others and their search. It is predicated on the assumption that we cannot understand others until we have understood ourselves. We cannot experience others' oppression until we are aware of the oppression in our own lives. It is the ultimate lesson that we have learned from Confucius, the Buddha, the Greek philosophers and the New Testament: "Know thyself."

A recent study of a group of persons involved in transcendental meditation, which emphasizes self-discovery and self-realization, listed the following characteristics as evident in the persons studied: restful alertness; clearer thinking; less discord, tension and hostility; enriched perception; and harmonious and fulfilling interpersonal relationships. Knowledge of oneself and one's culture has a liberating effect. One can respond more positively, without conflict, to the culture of others. It can be a spiritually nourishing and rewarding experience.

Edward F. Hall in *Beyond Culture* observes that "the cultural and psychological insight that is important for man (and woman) to accept is that denying culture can be as destructive as denying evil." We must come to terms with both. At least a part of the evil that besets us is the practice of ranking either persons, groups or cultures in reference to ourselves. Pluralism encourages us to face the fact that there are many roads to truth and no culture has the only map or is better equipped than others to search for it. "What is more, no one can tell another how to conduct that search."

Pluralism encourages a search for identity and an appreciation for that identity. The search for identity has serious implications for pluralism and for Christians, which we shall discuss in the next chapter.

# CHAPTER 6: RECALL/RESPONSE

## RECALL

"We can grow through meaningful encounter and dialogue with persons and groups who will not simply reinforce our prejudices, but will challenge our assumptions. When members of a majority cultural group are locked into their own cultural existence, they suffer, for they are deprived of many rich values that may come to them from authentic interaction with other cultural groupings."

"Pluralism encourages bi-cultural and multi-cultural identities. Encouragement of this development will give us not only a renewed respect for our own country with its many cultural and ethnic groups, but also an appreciation of true universalism, in which the merits and weaknesses of other belief systems can be more appropriately assessed because persons or groups deeply understand and appreciate more than one culture."

"At least a part of the evil that besets us is the practice of ranking either persons, groups or cultures in reference to ourselves."

"Characterized by openness, free access and mutual respect, pluralism allows persons and groups to discover the incredible richness and variety of other cultures and lifestyles and to borrow from one another as good neighbors always do. And it is a reciprocal process. It does not destroy the goodness and beauty of one . . . to supplant it with that of another."

## RESPONSE

(1) Pluralism (religious) has become a key word in mainline discussions about the church and its nature. But in your local church a group of evangelicals maintain that pluralism implies compromise of the faith. A pluralistic church, they say, will lead to an "apostate church"; besides, its polity is Unitarian and not Protestant. How can you establish dialogue in this issue? Does pluralism mean that the church is conceived of as a "theological cafeteria offering both poison and nourishment"? If that is not so, then why is it not so? Stage a meeting in your local church in which these issues are

debated. Be sure that at least two other points of view are represented. End the meeting before a decision can be made and discuss the dynamics of the discussion rather than focusing on the issues being discussed.

(2) Diana Chang, an Asian-American poet, has written of the experience of living in two cultures. Analyze one of her poems in which the poet struggles with the consciousness of the duality of being Chinese-American.

### OTHERNESS[19]

"Are you Chinese?
Are you American?"

I am fascinated

but other

anywhere

so it follows
                    (laconically)

I
must
be

Jewish

Leading to an eye-opener:
*real* Chinese in China
not feeling other,
                    not international
                    not cosmopolitan

are gentiles, no less

no wonder
I felt the way I did
in the crowd

not there

not here.

a) What does this say about identity?

b) What does this say about "home"?

c) What implications does it have for forms or questionnaires to be checked by persons who have to place an "X" in a box marked "other"? What color is "other"?

(3) In small groups, write a litany praising God for the diversity of peoples and cultures and the unity of humankind. Discuss the elements of the litany and then choose appropriate hymns and scripture to complete a brief worship service. Hymns and scripture should be discussed, analyzed and chosen to reflect the diversity of the universal church and our oneness in Christ. Intercessory prayer can be a part of the service of worship. Then share parts of each group's litany with the larger group for a closing worship experience.

# 7

# A COMMUNITY OF PILGRIMS

Christians are called to be pilgrims. From the call of Abraham to go from his home country and his kindred to another land, and throughout the Old and New Testaments, Christian identity is associated with being pilgrims who follow in faithful obedience wherever God leads. We leave friendly and familiar territory and venture toward unknown horizons. We have no fixed resting place—because we are not settlers but pilgrims. We are on a journey to find community. We follow God's leading.

We live in a day when transitions must be made from the avenues through which God has moved, to new ones. The settings for our efforts of faith must be transcended, and ways of releasing God's salvation in new arenas must be explored. A certain kind of person will be called for, if we are to move on to new territories—pilgrims and sojourners. Certain understandings of God's action and the church's calling will also be necessary if we are to move with God into a pluralistic society and a pluralistic world.

The ancient apologist in the *Epistle to Diognetius* expressed it well: "Christians inhabit their own land but as sojourners. They share in all things outwardly as citizens, and endure all things as strangers. Every foreign land is theirs, and every land is foreign." This same biblical imagery was picked up by the writer of one of our powerful hymns: "Guide me, O Thou great Jehovah, Pilgrim through this barren land."

## En Route, With Roots

While the writer of Ephesians says, "So then you are no longer strangers and sojourners" in relation to God (Ephesians 2:19), the writers of Hebrews and 1 Peter say Christians are to continue as "strangers and pilgrims" in relation to the world. These writers were

119

following the practice of the ancient Hebrews. In their earlier recital of the mighty acts of God, they remembered what happened to them as sojourners. "A wandering Aramean was my father; and he went down into Egypt and sojourned there" (Deuteronomy 26:5). The credal formulation no doubt referred to such figures as Abraham. After years of travel, Abraham finally took up residence in the land God had promised to give him. And yet he felt he should pay for a plot of land he had found in which to bury his beloved Sarah. Although the neighbors felt the land was his to take, Abraham insisted on paying for it because, he said, "I am a stranger and a sojourner among you" (Genesis 23:4). The writer of 1 Peter addresses the Christians with the words: "Beloved, I beseech you as aliens and exiles" (1 Peter 2:11).

Centuries later, as the story has it, King David claimed the same identity. As death approached, he called upon the people for gifts to construct a House of God. In his prayer to God he said, "But who am I, and what is my people, that we should be able thus to offer willingly? For all things come from thee, and of thy own have we given thee. For we are strangers before thee, and sojourners, as all our fathers were; our days on the earth are like a shadow, and there is no abiding" (1 Chronicles 29:14-15; see too Leviticus 25:23). We read other prayers in Psalms where the devout Jews called themselves pilgrims and strangers (Psalms 39:12; 119:19). Besides these specific instances of actual uses of the terms "pilgrims," "strangers," "sojourners," "aliens," and "exiles," the very contours of their faith depict them as a transient people. Again and again, they told new stories and reshaped old ones because changing circumstances forced updating as they moved through history from place to place.

With such a longstanding practice as this, it should not surprise us that the Christians who called themselves the "New Israel" would also see themselves as strangers, pilgrims and sojourners on the earth. For about 300 years the local congregations in the Greek-speaking communities called themselves sojourners or exiles (*paroikos*, in Greek). No doubt they recalled the early band of disciples who moved about with the One who said, "Foxes have holes, and birds of the air have nests; but the Son of man has nowhere to lay his head" (Matthew 8:20). And as they met in hideaways and catacombs, they saw themselves in company with those who "went about in skins of sheep and goats, destitute, afflicted, ill-treated—of whom the world was not worthy—wandering over deserts and mountains, and in dens and caves of the earth" (Hebrews 11:37-38). If in those early centuries the local church was called, more often than not, the "sojourners," "pilgrims" or *paroikoi*, the church universal was likely to be called *ecclesia*, i.e., the ones who were called out to be separated (1 Corinthians 6:17).

These excursions into the identity of the ancient Hebrews, the New Testament Christians and the early church reveal a persisting identity of the people who lived with the God of biblical faith. They found they were pilgrims or sojourners, not settlers, aliens even in the land of their birth. If their God was a God on the move and therefore could not be "frozen" into images and statues, it was natural the people of God would call themselves sojourners and pilgrims. The contemporary people of God can be nothing less. But something comparable to a John Bunyan may be needed again. For centuries Christians had come to think of pilgrims as those who went to a certain place to pay homage to the God who had done miraculous things at that place in the past. After Bunyan wrote *Pilgrim's Progress* in the seventeenth century, it was no longer possible to think of pilgrims in that same way, but as those who were moving ahead toward ever-new manifestations of God in unexpected circumstances. The shift of consciousness which his book signalled and even fostered turned people from looking back to looking forward. A comparable shift in consciousness will be necessary if we are to move with our Living God, whose seat on the ancient altar remained empty because God could not be tied to it, or even contained in the temple. There was more to create, more to redeem.

The biblical people of God who saw themselves en route, however, had roots. As we continue, in the grand tradition of Luke, trying to make it possible for God's work to emerge through persons previously overlooked, individuals with their own unique cultural heritage and their unique locus in society, we see ourselves in need of faith, or rootage. Being different, overlooked or oppressed does not necessarily mean we will be the avenues of God's new work of salvation, healing and liberation. Paul may have made it a specialty in his ministry to release God's actions through persons who had not known God's work, but he warned these Gentiles against pride. He reminded the Gentiles they were "wild olive branches" grafted into the strong olive tree which represented earlier avenues of God's work.

121

But if some of the branches were broken off, and you, a wild olive shoot, were grafted in their place to share the richness of the olive tree, do not boast over the branches. If you do boast, remember it is not you that support the root, but the root that supports you. . . . They were broken off because of their unbelief, but you stand fast only through faith. So do not become proud, but stand in awe. (Romans 11:17-21)

God will not choose to work through us simply because we initiate a novel form of ministry, or are among those who need it. Paul understood the critical role which faith played.

## The Mission of God

God's action is a clue to the church's calling. That is, we are called to follow God, who shapes the ministry of the church. For this exploration into the mission of God, let us look at two aspects of the Trinity: God as Creator and the God in Jesus Christ.

### Creation and Our Participation

Faith in God as Creator enables us to live with the particularities of history, and to recognize them as participants in the actions of creation. Existing human communities as they have emerged in history must be affirmed—whether blacks from Africa or German immigrants from the Old Country. Thus, we must see the development of distinctive human communities—whether social, economic, cultural, political or ethnic communities—as good. The very act of structuring the church to meet and work with communities defined in particular ways by the exigencies of history or geography is our way of acknowledging and affirming those communities.

What God is creating in the historical process is to be seen as good, whether ethnically defined communities or any other subgroup. All communities are invited to join the Creator in the continuing work of creation. Humankind is thus co-creator with the Creator. Thus, when we speak of God as Creator, we are affirming the particularities of creation, and the invitation extended to humankind to be participants in creative actions.

### Incarnated Christ and Christian Ministry

It has been traditional within the church to divide the works of God into creation and redemption. Thus we turn from creation to the divine qualities known in the experience of salvation. Although the Creator God is not excluded from the efforts of salvation or redemption, the focus shifts to the God known in Jesus.

One interpretation of the actions of God in Jesus has been as "Incarnation." That is, God enfleshed himself in the person of a Jew. This God acts through a marginalized person, working to save people from their sin, and from its consequences in various forms of evil, including illness, possession by evil spirits, and exploitations. While this God reaches out to redeem others in and through a person, resistance arises among those who have something to lose. The conflict leads to the crucifixion of Jesus. But one who lives in faithful service with such vulnerability releases new life, as we see in Jesus' resurrection. The same person is not simply brought back to life, but is transformed. The servant of salvation becomes the Lord of Hosts over the "hosts of lords" who had prevailed over humanity and possessed them. While the words and deeds of Jesus before his death and resurrection instruct his followers in the way they should live, his death and resurrection also indicate how redemption is accomplished (Luke 9:23).

Although reaching out and into the world of others as they live is an integral part of this model of ministries, the crucifixion which is so central to our understanding of Jesus suggests something more. It suggests that we take into our person the evil which the world can unleash upon servants of God, as we, like Jesus, move in and try to bind the "strong man" (Luke 11:21-22).

A style for mission during Euro-American expansionism and colonization spoke of the missionaries' offering of possessions and superior knowledge to others. It emphasized reaching and giving. The flow of life, healing and light went from the missionizing church to the objects of mission. As we advance further into a period of Euro-American decline, the church which is identified with the sometimes deceptive image of those past glories will find the need to live the faith in very different ways. We will need to learn how we can deal redemptively with what we take in, not only what we give out; we will be called to work constructively with what we absorb, not in the way we penetrate other cultures with what we see as the light. We will need models for ministry that involve receptivity alongside of giving.

Nothing offers us more hope and guidance for service under such circumstances than the cross. The crucifixion tells us of a God who works redemptively by what is taken in. In the case of the ancient Israelites, what was taken in may have been evils, in punishment for the people's own sins, but when double was meted out for their sins, a voice emerged to comfort the people and speak of the suffering servant (Isaiah 40 and 53). In the case of Jesus, we see the righteous one suffering ignominiously and yet redemptively, and by what he suffers, being transformed.

Thus, one who lives in a culture, among a particular people, may have something to teach and good deeds to perform. That is the lesson of the Incarnation. But integral to that service is the taking in of all that the person's very own people can subject that person to, including death. Through that death is released a new life. The people and their culture are transformed. On the one hand, we can find continuity in the one who is transformed, but, on the other hand, we find discontinuity. To be a good Christian means we continue as good Jews, as sojourners who are en route but retain their roots. We made their Bible our Bible, and continue many of their teachings. But Judaism is so transformed that Jesus produced Christians and the church which replaced the temple.

As H. Richard Niebuhr taught us in his study of *Christ and Culture*, Christ may be *against cultures* at a number of points, and yet Christ can be *of cultures* in that he is expressive of them. Further, Christ can be *above cultures*—fulfilling what cultures by themselves could not fulfill—or Christ can be *in paradoxical relations to cultures* by allowing cultures to be themselves and setting alongside them another set of values that are equally as valid as the cultural ones, yet appearing to contradict them.

The relationship which we have been exploring between Christ and cultures in this chapter is the fifth traditional option which Niebuhr describes: Christ the *transformer of culture*. A development of this interpretation of Christ in terms of a culture suggests that the transformer lives in, with, and among the transformer's own people and seeks to cleanse them of evil by teaching and deeds. When that work prompts the transformer's death, the transformer takes in all the evil which could not be eradicated by the teaching and good deeds; through the ensuing resurrection, new life is released. This is not resuscitation of the old, but a transformation—sin and evil are taken out of a given people and they are made whole. It is clear, from this vision of that final moment, that persons will continue the identities which they had on this earth, but they will be fully redeemed from the sin and evils that distorted them. This interpretation of the word of God in Jesus as the Christ is that of an irreversible process of redemption which God has set in motion. Setbacks can occur, but over the long haul, a light has shone in the darkness and the darkness is unable to overcome it (John 1:5).

## The Church and the World

Many of the churches in North America are small rural churches, many others are suburban, but their lives are shaped by the same national and international forces that affect urban areas. And the reality of a scarcity of resources is finally dawning upon the American population.

Indeed, we are one world, whether we perceive that on the conscious level or not. But it is our task as the Body of Christ to work consciously and intentionally toward the emerging norm set by the World Council of Churches: a just, sustainable and participatory society. That must be a conscious part of our outreach ministries. This has strong implications for the way we have usually viewed "missions." No longer can American churches be seen as missionizing churches, but rather churches in *partnership* with churches of the Third World—receiving as well as giving.

One might say that a local church unaware of this interdependence is globally deprived. We must see the world as a unity. The presence of many ethnic minorities in the church and in America in general provides an opportunity to experience with persons "at home" the reality of our global society, which requires that we seriously embrace pluralism and celebrate our diversity.

The church exists to continue the ministry of Jesus in the world. That ministry is one of servanthood, of caring, healing, confronting the powers and principalities and seeking to establish the rule of a righteous God on earth. That must be true of the church's ministry wherever God's people are—in cities and suburbs, in hamlets and villages, in rural areas and small towns. The question must be asked of the church's ministry: Does the program, project, activity, ministry continue the Master's ministry?

It is not for ourselves but for others that we seek to be servants, sensitive to the hurts and ills of the world, serving the needs of those who have been forgotten, hearing the cries for help and following the lead of God, being advocates for those who have no advocate, becoming a voice for the voiceless and providing a refuge for those who need sanctuary. Our ministry must be seen as created by the pattern of incarnation of our Lord.

## Jesus: Model of Ministry

This model is Jesus as Founder of a new way of ministry, especially as depicted in the Gospel according to Luke. One might contrast it to the story of Jesus' work recorded in the Gospel of Matthew.

According to Matthew, God's work of salvation in Jesus happened through a Jew of the Jews. The writer emphasizes, through various means, the image of Jesus as the fulfillment of everything the Jews had been looking for. He cites prophecies to show how the birth, trip to Egypt (like the one Moses took), service, and death of Jesus were predicted in Jewish literature. Even the Sermon on the Mount is one of the five bodies of teaching material in Matthew, reminiscent, we are told by some, of the five books of Moses; and Jesus delivers this sermon from the mountain, just as Moses delivered the Law from Sinai. This was unlike the setting of the sermon on the plain for the same teaching summarized differently in Luke (Luke 6:17ff).

We are told by Matthew that Jesus' work had his fellow Jews primarily in mind. When he sends the disciples on a mission, Jesus says, "Go nowhere among the Gentiles, and enter no town of the Samaritans, but go rather to the lost sheep of the house of Israel." In Luke what seems to be a report of the same event contains no such restriction. In another contrast, on one occasion Luke shows Jesus' openness to the Samaritans, whom Matthew says Jesus had prohibited from his field of mission. According to Luke, Jesus "sent messengers ahead of him, who went and entered a village of the Samaritans" (Luke 9:52). And in a report of the evangelistic work of the witness, Luke reports that Jesus cited the Gentiles as models of conversion and Jews as samples of condemnation.

Woe to you, Chorazin! woe to you, Bethsaida! for if the mighty works done in you had been done in Tyre and Sidon, they would have repented long ago, sitting in sackcloth and ashes. But it shall be more tolerable in the judgment for Tyre and Sidon than for you. And you, Capernaum, will you be exalted to heaven? You shall be brought down to Hades. (Luke 10:13-15)

(Compare that with Matthew 15:21-28, "It is not fair to take the children's bread and throw it to the dogs," with reference to a person from that region. Luke 4:24-28 conveys the same message as Luke 10:13.)

We know of Luke's references to the poor, the Gentiles, the Samaritans, women and the handicapped as the focal points of salvation in his stories. The point seems to be that the process of salvation has moved from those associated with it in the past and begins to work through others! The Samaritans, for example, are models of faith and service, as in the story of the leper who returned to offer thanks (Luke 17:11-19). The story of the Good Samaritan is told only by Luke (Luke 10:30-37).

A vivid illustration appears in the second book associated with Luke, namely, the Acts of the Apostles. We find it in that long speech which Stephen delivered before he was stoned to death. The length of his speech was sufficient reason to make people angry; but the conclusion was intolerable. He levelled severe charges against the religious leaders of Jewish history. "You stiff-necked people, uncircumcised in heart and ears, you always resist the Holy Spirit" (Acts 7:51).

What were they resisting? A survey of his speech will tell the answer. It rehearses a sketchy history of the Jewish people. He highlights the efforts of Abraham (vs. 3-9); Joseph (9-16); Moses (17-44); and David and Solomon (45-50). Several themes here are worth noting for outreach ministries.

First, the rejected are often the ones who are leading the people of God into salvation. Joseph, the rejected brother, led his family out of famine to plenty; Moses, the rejected liberator, led his people through the deep waters and the dry deserts toward the promised land. Second, notice where these deliverers encounter God. Abraham meets God in Mesopotamia, outside Israel; Moses constructs a "tent of witness" in the wilderness. The tent is the place where the people of God encounter the divine, and was called at times "tent of meeting." That meeting happened outside the temple! And even when David and Solomon built the temple, notice what God says about the temple:

127

Heaven is my throne, and earth my footstool.
What house will you build for me, says the Lord,
or what is the place of my rest? Did not my hand
make all these things? (Acts 7:49-50)

No building could contain the divine presence. God would appear outside the sacred precincts of the temple.

What do we make of these stories from Luke concerning the work of Jesus and the witness of the early church? Salvation comes through Gentiles, Samaritans, the poor, women and the handicapped. It is as if he were saying that while Jesus may have been the epitome of the highest ancient religion, he released the process of salvation through the outsiders, the rejected and neglected ones. Matthew wanted to make Jesus look like a good Jew, who did his work first among the Jews before his disciples would "make disciples of all nations," (Matthew 28:19). For Luke, God came in Jesus to set loose healing through new persons, through new cultures, through new resources outside those which had been effective in the past. Those who identify themselves with this Jesus will therefore not surprisingly find themselves becoming avenues of the same kind of actions of God.

Ivan Illich has observed that "neither efficiency nor comfort nor affluence are criteria for the quality of change. Only the reaction of the human heart to change indicates the objective value of that change." We seek change—not simply change as designed by the dominant group, but change in a developmental sense, i.e., through respect for the right of each group to self-determination and providing self-reliance. Our program must not reduce bewildered individuals into dependence but must respect the right to self-determination and empowerment.

This means sharing in leadership and in redistributing resources. It means giving attention to radical alternatives to power; analyses of societal trends different from those now deduced by common denominators; and including those now excluded from the centers of power in the determining of priorities, programs and the use of resources. Our ministries must enable the powerless to have power. Our ministries must abstain from unilaterally engineering the shape of the future for those who have no power. Our advocacy stance must enable those who are voiceless to speak about their own lives as they determine what their future is to be.

We are the church being the church. We are sojourners and pilgrims struggling to be faithful. Our vocation is to finish the work the Master began. We point to a kingdom which is visible to us and which we seek to make visible to others in fulfilling our Lord's mandate, without any ulterior, self-serving motives. We are seeking to be faithful, travelling light, having laid aside the weight, "looking to Jesus the pioneer and perfecter of our faith" (Hebrews 12:2).

# NOTES

## Chapter 1

[1]Chief Seattle, "The Unforked Message of Chief Seattle," trans. Wm. Arrowsmith in *Bicentennial Broadside: Bicentennial Resources for Churches*, Dept. of Publication Service, National Council of Churches, New York, N.Y.

[2]Quoted in Thomas F. Gossett, *Race: The History of an Idea in America* (New York: Schocken Books, 1965), p. 179.

[3]*Ibid.*, p. 179.

[4]Quoted in Charles Abrams, *Forbidden Neighbors* (New York: Harper & Brothers, 1955), p. 30.

[5]*Ibid.*, p. 32.

[6]Raymond Leslie Buell, "The Development of the Anti-Japanese Agitation in the United States," *Political Science Quarterly* (New York: Ginn & Co., vol. 37, no. 4, December 1922), pp. 621, 623.

[7]George Tuttle, "Racial Myths and Racial Hatred," in *Peace, Power, Protest*, ed. Donald Evans (Toronto: Ryerson Press, 1967), p. 139.

[8]Quoted in Robert N. Bellah, *The Broken Covenant* (New York: Seabury Press, 1975), p. 87.

[9]*Ibid.*, p. 88.

[10]Kyle Haselden, *Death of a Myth* (New York: Friendship Press, 1964), p. 73

[11]James M. Jones, *Prejudice and Racism* (Reading, Mass.: Addison-Wesley, 1972), p. 137.

## Chapter 2

[1]Three races were generally accepted, although others divided the human race into 5 groups and some went so far as to identify 17 groups and 29 races.

[2]Jensen, Arthur R., *Educability and Group Differences* (New York: Harper and Row, 1973), p. 363.

[3]Gordon Allport, *The ABCs of Scapegoating* (New York: Anti-Defamation League of B'nai Brith, 1979).

[4] Ben Hecht, *A Guide for the Bedevilled* (New York: Charles Scribner's Sons, 1944), p. 31).

[5]Allport, *op. cit.*, p. 42.

[6]*Ibid.*, p. 408.

[7]Stokely Carmichael and C.V. Hamilton, *Black Power: The Politics of Liberation in America* (New York: Vintage Books, 1967), p. 4.

[8]James M. Jones, *Prejudice and Racism* (Reading, Mass.: Addison-Wesley, 1972), p. 4.

[9]Bishop Walter Sullivan, "Strangers and Aliens No Longer," *Origins,* Vol. 9, No. 16, Oct. 4, 1979, p. 243.

[10]Isaac Bivens, "Institutional Racism," Board of Global Ministries, World Division, United Methodist Church, 1979.

[11]Dick Gregory, *The Light Side: The Dark Side,* Poppy Industries Album, 1969.

[12]Jones, *op. cit.,* p. 131.

[13]Knowles and Prewitt, *Institutional Racism in America* (Englewood Cliffs, N.J.: Prentice-Hall, 1969).

## Chapter 3

[1]Joseph Barndt, *Liberating Our White Ghetto* (Minneapolis: Augsburg Publishing House, 1972), pp. 79-80.

[2]Quoted in Robert N. Bellah, *The Broken Covenant* (New York: Seabury Press, 1975), p. 76. See his discussion of "Salvation and Success," Chapter 3, pp. 61-86, for a clear and persuasive delineation of the development of the vision of religion and success as a single enterprise in American society.

[3]Barndt, *op. cit.,* p. 104.

[4]C. Vann Woodward, *The Irony of Southern History* (Indianapolis: Bobbs-Merrill, 1953).

[5]David W. Briddell, "Concern for Human Culture," *The Interpreter,* March 1973, pp. 3-6.

[6]William Greenbaum, "America in Search of a New Ideal: An Essay on the Rise of Pluralism," *Howard Educational Review,* Vol. 44, No. 3, August 1974, p. 431.

[7]Israel Zangwill, *The Melting Pot: Drama in Four Acts* (New York: Macmillan Co., 1921), pp. 35ff.

[8]Octavio Paz, "Eroticism and Gastrosophy," *Daedalus,* 101, p. 74. See the whole article, pp. 67-86, for a fuller discussion.

[9]See Milton M. Gordon, *Assimilation in American Life* (London: Oxford University Press, 1964), pp. 85ff., for a discussion of the theory of "Anglo-Conformity," which he says "demanded the complete renunciation of the immigrant's ancestral culture in favor of the behavior and values of the Anglo-Saxon core group."

[10]See Michael Novak, *The Rise of the Unmeltable Ethnics* (New York: Macmillan, 1971); Peter Schrag, *The Decline of the WASP* (New York: Simon and Schuster, 1970); William Greenbaum, *op. cit.,* pp. 411-440; also Joseph Barndt, *op. cit.,* offers a passionate personal plea based on his experience as an "imprisoned, white, male, middle class American" (Protestant); and in Donald Shockley, *Free, White and Christian* (Nashville: Abingdon Press, 1975), see especially pp. 48-79, where the author discusses the incongruity between national self-understanding and social reality and calls for a "new white consciousness."

[11]Greenbaum, *op. cit.*, p. 426.

[12]*Ibid.*

[13]*Ethnic Minorities in the United Methodist Church* (Nashville, Tenn.: Disciple Resources, 1976), p. 1.

[14]Barndt, *op. cit.*, p. 26.

[15]*Ibid.*, pp. 25-26.

[16]In Symposium, "Church and State in the U.S.A. and Canada," before the Religious Education Association of the United States and Canada. *Religious Education,* May-June 1974, p. 378.

[17]See Joseph Barndt and George Barbek, "International Consciousness: Education for Awareness and Action," Report of an Action/Research Project for the Division of World Mission and Ecumenism, Lutheran Church in America, May 1973.

[18]Edward T. Hall, *Beyond Culture* (Garden City, N.Y.: Anchor Press/Doubleday, 1976), p. 35.

[19]Greenbaum, *op. cit.*, p. 412.

[20]*Ibid.*

[21]*Ibid.* (italics added).

[22]*Ibid.*

[23]*Ibid.*, p. 423.

[24]*Ibid.*, p. 431.

[25]*Ibid.*, p. 438.

[26]*Ibid.*

[27]*Ibid.*, p. 440.

[28]*Ibid.*

[29]E. Digsby Baltzell, *The Protestant Establishment* (New York: Vintage Books, 1966), Preface, page x.

[30]Greenbaum, *op. cit.*, p. 427.

[31]Harold Cruse, *The Crisis of the Negro Intellectual* (New York: William Morrow & Co., Inc., 1967), p. 456 (Italics added).

## Chapter 4

[1]"Towards a New Style of Living," Report of Section VI, *The Uppsala Report,* 1968 (Geneva: World Council of Churches, 1973), p. 87.

[2]Emil Brunner, *Man in Revolt,* trans. Olive Wyon (London, 1939), p. 333.

[3]Waldo Beach, "A Theological Analysis of Race Relations," in *Faith and Ethics,* ed. Paul Ramsey (New York: Harper & Row, 1957), p. 211.

[4]George D. Kelsey, *Racism and the Christian Understanding of Man* (New York: Charles Scribner's Sons, 1965), p. 27.

[5]Beach, *op. cit.*, p. 213.

[6]I owe this point to George Kelsey (see Kelsey, *op. cit.*, pp. 25-26). While the development here is somewhat different from his, the essential statement is his.

[7]Quoted in John Vincent, *The Race Race* (London: SCM Press, 1970), p. 39. See also *A Charter for Racial Justice Policies in an Interdependent Global Community*, Women's Division, Board of Global Ministries, the United Methodist Church, April 1978. Printed in *Of Life and Hope: Toward Effective Witness in Human Rights*, ed. Mia Adjali (New York: Friendship Press, 1979), pp. 25-27.

[8]The lawyer's question is really a repetition of the injunction in Lev. 19:18. It provides Jesus with an opportunity to present a theological meaning of "neighbor" which he gives in the Parable of the Good Samaritan (Luke 10:25-37). As Harrell F. Beck points out: "Superficially the parable suggests that Jesus would have his followers recognize their neighbors as those in need of services . . . rather, it was the man who had compassion who 'proved neighbor to the man who fell among the robbers'" (vs. 36). Beck further points out that the meaning of "neighbor" in this setting is seen as those fellow beings who come forth to do good in a variety of ways and join Christ in the fellowship of suffering humanity (cf. Matt. 25:31-46). The meaning of "neighbor" in Jesus' answer "extends the term 'neighbor' until it is essentially coextensive with 'mankind' [sic]. This wider interpretation belongs to the term in the rest of the New Testament. Both Paul (Rom. 13:9) and James (James 2:8) regarded the commandment: 'You shall love your neighbor as yourself,' as the royal law and, in a sense, the summary of the law." See Harrell F. Beck, "Neighbor" in *The Interpreter's Dictionary of the Bible* (Nashville: Abingdon Press, 1962), p. 535.

[9]*Ibid.*

[10]C.E.B. Cranfield, "Love" in Richardson, *Theological Word Book*, p. 134.

[11]Paul Tillich, *Love, Power and Justice* (New York: Oxford University Press, 1960), p. 49.

[12]*Ibid.*, p. 11 (italics added).

[13]See Paulo Freire's discussion on the conditions for dialogue in Chapter 3 of his book, *Pedagogy of the Oppressed*, trans. Myra Bergman Ramos (New York: Herder and Herder, 1970), especially pp. 75-82.

[14]Nathan Wright, Jr., *Black Power and Urban Unrest* (New York: Hawthorn Books, 1967), p. 6.

[15]Quoted in Kyle Haselden, *Mandate for White Christians* (Richmond: Knox Press, 1966), p. 84.

[16]This phrase is borrowed from a study done in 1978 by the National Urban League, New York City, titled "The Illusion of Black Progress."

[17]For an illuminating discussion on the relationship between sexism and racism, see Robert Terry's "The White Male Club." *Racism/Sexism: Where Are We?*, a reprint by Organizational Leadership, Inc., 512 S. Main St., Adrian, Michigan.

[18]Those who maintain the "illusion of progress" cite the rise in the ratio of black/white incomes as proof of progress. They fail to point out that (a) the gap in buying power has expanded; and (b) "black families own less than 2 percent of the nation's wealth, and about 70 percent of the little they own is in the form of the wealth that is least associated with power, namely, equity in a home." *Ibid.*, p. 3.

[19]Equality is used here to mean "oneness" and not "sameness." George Kelsey has pointed out that to speak of "equality of opportunity" in matters of race is "little more than a fiction because it has proposed equality of opportunity without equality of person. . . . It fails to take into account the spiritual and psychological quality of life." See George D. Kelsey, "The Ethico-Cultural Revolution in American Race Relations," *Religion in Life*, Abingdon Press, Nashville, Tennessee, Summer 1957, p. 341. Christian ethics, and indeed the whole of the biblical faith, maintains that we are members of one human family with a spiritual affinity which all should share with one another and are not merely persons deriving benefits (rights, things) from an organized society. Equality as a goal, in the latter sense, could be achieved without touching the problem of the divided human family—our major concern here.

[20]Rudolf Bultmann, *Existence and Faith*, trans. and ed. Schubert M. Ogden (New York: Meridian Books, 1960), p. 176.

[21]Emil Brunner, *The Christian Doctrine of Creation and Redemption*, Vol. II, *Dogmatics*, trans. Olive Wyon (Philadelphia: Westminster Press, 1952), pp. 58-59.

[22]Michael Novak, *A Theology for Radical Politics* (New York: Herder and Herder, 1969), p. 40.

**Chapter 5**

[1]Gayraud Wilmore, "The New Context of Black Theology in the United States," *Occasional Bulletin of Missionary Research*, October 1977.

[2]Roy Sano, *Redeeming the Seminaries: The Promise of Ethnic Centers* (Madison, N.J.: Multi-Ethnic Center Press, 1980).

[3]"Submission of the Committee on International Affairs of the Canadian Council of Churches in Response to the Government Paper on Canadian Foreign Policy," Toronto, Feb. 1971.

[4]Franklin H. Littell, *From State Church to Pluralism: A Protestant Interpretation of Religion in American History* (Chicago: Aldine, 1962), p. xv.

## Chapter 6

[1]See William James, *The Varieties of Religious Experience* (New York: The Modern Library, 1929); and William James, *A Pluralistic Universe* (Folcroft, Pa.: Folcroft Library Editions, 1973); and Randolph S. Bourne, "Transnational America," *The Atlantic Monthly*, 118 (1916), pp. 86-97.

[2]Horace M. Kallen, *Cultural Pluralism and the American Idea* (Philadelphia: University of Pennsylvania Press, 1956), p. 55.

[3]*Ibid.*, p. 100.

[4]Kallen, *op. cit.*, p. 46. Kallen's first use of the term "cultural pluralism" was in 1915 in an article in *The Nation* under the title "Democracy versus the Melting Pot." Here he vigorously rejected the usefulness of both concepts as models and proposed another model emphasizing cultural pluralism. The statement in the reference cited represents a development over 45 years of work, which he spent teaching and developing essays and other writings dealing with the theme of American multiple-group life. Most of his years were spent teaching at the New School for Social Research.

[5]Orlando Patterson, "On Guilt, Relativism and Black-White Relations," *The American Scholar*, 43 (1973-1974), p. 129.

[6]Patterson, *op. cit.*, p. 127.

[7]*Ibid., op. cit.*, p. 127.

[8]See Stein and Hill, *The Ethnic Imperative* (University Park: Pennsylvania State Univ. Press, 1977), p. 264. See pp. 262-266 for a fuller statement of this argument.

[9]*Ibid.*, p. 266.

[10]*Ibid.*

[11]See Orlando Patterson, *Ethnic Chauvinism: The Reactionary Impulse* (New York: Stein and Day, 1977), pp. 223-229.

[12]See Galatians 2 and Acts 15.

[13]For an enlightening discussion on the subject see *Social Justice and Preferential Treatment: Women and Racial Minorities in Education and Business*, ed. William T. Blackstone and Robert D. Heslep (Athens: Univ. of Georgia Press, 1977). The book is a compilation of the formal addresses given at a conference titled "The Policy of Compensatory Justice for Women and Racial Minorities in Education and Business" held at the University of Georgia. The work contains arguments on both sides of the issues by leading scholars in the fields of law and philosophy, businessmen and academic administrators.

[14]*Ibid.*, p. 3. See the discussion of thi  thesis on pp. 16-32 in the chapter titled "The University and the Case for Preferential Treatment."

[15]Michael Novak, *A Theology for Radical Politics* (New York: Herder and Herder, 1969), p. xvi.

[16]Quoted in E. Digsby Baltzell, *The Protestant Establishment* (New York: Vintage Books, 1966), p. 197.

[17]Roy Sano, *Redeeming the Seminaries: The Promise of Ethnic Centers* (Madison, N.J.: Multi-Ethnic Center Press, 1980), p. 9.

[18]*Ibid.*, p. 12.

[19]Diana Chang, "Otherness," *Asian-American Heritage: An Anthology of Prose and Poetry*, ed. David Hsin-Fu Wand (New York: Washington Square Press, 1974), pp. 135-136. Copyright ©1974 by Diana Chang. Used by permission.

# BIBLIOGRAPHY

Abrams, Charles, *Forbidden Neighbors*. New York: Harper and Brothers, 1955.

Allport, Gordon, *The Nature of Prejudice*. Cambridge, Mass.: Addison-Wesley Publishing Co., 1954.

Baltzell, E. Digsby, *The Protestant Establishment*. New York: Vintage Books, 1966.

Barndt, Joseph, *Liberating Our White Ghetto*. Minneapolis: Augsburg Publishing House, 1972.

Barndt, Joseph and Barbek, George, "International Consciousness: Education for Awareness and Action," Report of an Action/Research Project for the Division of World Mission and Ecumenism, Lutheran Church in America, May 1973.

Beach, Waldo, "A Theological Analysis of Race Relations," *Faith and Ethics*, ed. Paul Ramsey. New York: Harper and Row, 1957.

Beck, Harrell, "Neighbor," *The Interpreter's Dictionary of the Bible*. Nashville: Abingdon Press, 1962.

Bellah, Robert N., *The Broken Covenant*. New York: Seabury Press, 1975.

Bivens, Isaac, "Institutional Racism," Board of Global Ministries, World Division, United Methodist Church, 1979.

Blackstone, William T., and Heslep, Robert D., eds., *Social Justice and Preferential Treatment: Women and Racial Minorities in Education and Business*. Athens: University of Georgia Press, 1977.

Bourne, Randolph S., "Trans-National America," *The Atlantic Monthly*, vol. 118, 1916.

Briddell, David W., "Concern for Human Culture," *The Interpreter*, March 1973.

Brunner, Emil, "Dogmatics," *Man in Revolt*, trans. Olive Wyon. New York: Scribner, 1939.

_____ *The Christian Doctrine of Creation and Redemption, Dogmatics*, vol. II, trans. Olive Wyon, Philadelphia: Westminster Press, 1952.

Buell, Raymond Leslie, "The Development of the Anti-Japanese Agitation in the United States," *Political Science Quarterly*. New York: Ginn & Co., vol. 37, no. 4, December, 1922.

Bultmann, Rudolf, *Existence and Faith*, trans. and ed. Schubert M. Ogden. New York: Meridian Books, 1960.

Canadian Council of Churches, "Submission of the Committee on International Affairs of the Canadian Council of Churches in Response to the Government: Paper on Canadian Foreign Policy," Canadian Council of Churches, February 1971.

Carmichael, Stokely and Hamilton, C.V., *Black Power: The Politics of Liberation in America*. New York: Vintage Books, 1967.

Commager, Henry Steele, "The Ambiguous American," *New York Times Magazine, The New York Times,* May 3, 1964.

Cranfield, C. E. B., "Love," in *Theological Word Book,* ed. Allan Richardson. London: SCM Press, 1950.

Cruse, Harold, *The Crisis of the Negro Intellectual.* New York: William Morrow & Company, 1967.

Disciple Resources, *Ethnic Minorities in the United Methodist Church.* Nashville: Disciple Resources, 1976.

Freire, Paulo, *Pedagogy of the Oppressed,* trans. Myra Bergman Ramos. New York: Herder & Herder, 1970.

Gordon, Milton M., *Assimilation in American Life.* London: Oxford University Press, 1964.

Gossett, Thomas F., *Race: The History of an Idea in America.* New York: Schocken Books, 1965.

Greenbaum, William, "America in Search for a New Ideal: An Essay on the Rise of Pluralism," *Howard Educational Review,* vol. 44, no. 3, August 1974.

Gregory, Dick, *The Light Side: The Dark Side,* Poppy Industries Album, 1969.

Hall, Edward T., *Beyond Culture.* Garden City, N.Y.: Anchor Press/Doubleday 1976.

Haselden, Kyle, *Death of a Myth.* New York: Friendship Press, 1964.

——————— *Mandate for White Christians.* Richmond: Knox Press, 1966.

Hecht, Ben, *A Guide for the Bedevilled.* New York: Charles Scribner's Sons, 1944.

James, William, *A Pluralistic Universe.* Folcroft, Pa.: Folcroft Library Editions, 1972.

——————— *The Varieties of Religious Experience.* New York: The Modern Library, 1929.

Jensen, Arthur R., *Educability and Group Differences.* New York: Harper and Row, 1973.

Jones, James M., *Prejudice and Racism.* Reading, Mass.: Addison-Wesley, 1972.

Kallen, Horace M., *Cultural Pluralism and the American Idea.* Philadelphia: University of Pennsylvania Press, 1956.

Kelsey, George D., "The Ethico-Cultural Revolution in American Race Relations," *Religion in Life.* Nashville: Abingdon Press, 1957.

——————— *Racism and the Christian Understanding of Man.* New York: Charles Scribner's Sons, 1965.

Knowles and Prewitt, *Institutional Racism in America.* Englewood Cliffs, N.J.: Prentice-Hall, 1969.

Littell, Franklin H., *From State Church to Pluralism: Protestant Interpretation of Religion in American History.* Chicago: Aldine, 1962.

National Urban League, *The Illusion of Black Progress*. New York: National Urban League, 1978.

Novak, Michael, *The Rise of the Unmeltable Ethnics*. New York: Macmillan, 1971.
—————————— *A Theology for Radical Politics*. New York: Herder & Herder, 1969.

Patterson, Orlando, "On Guilt, Relativism and Black-White Relations," *The American Scholar*, vol. 43, 1973-1974.

Paz, Octavio, "Eroticism and Gastrosophy," *Daedalus*, vol. 101, 1972.

Sano, Roy I., *Redeeming the Seminaries: The Promise of Ethnic Centers*. Madison, N.J.: Multi-Ethnic Center Press, 1980.

Schrag, Peter, *The Decline of the WASP*. New York: Simon & Schuster, 1970.

Seattle, Chief, "The Unforked Message of Chief Seattle," trans. William Arrowsmith in *Bicentennial Broadside: Bicentennial Resources for Churches*, Department of Publication Service, National Council of Churches, New York, N.Y.

Shockley, Donald, *Free, White and Christian*. Nashville: Abingdon Press, 1975.

Sowell, Thomas, "Myths about Minorities," *Commentary*, August, 1979.

Sullivan, Bishop Walter, "Strangers and Aliens No Longer," *Origins*, vol. 9, no. 16, October 4, 1979.

Terry, Robert, "The White Male Club," *Racism/Sexism: Where Are We?* Adrian, Mich.: Organizational Leadership, Inc.

Tillich, Paul, *Love, Power and Justice*. New York: Oxford University Press, 1960.

van den Berghe, Pierre, *Race and Racism: A Comparative Perspective*. New York: Wiley, 1967.

Vincent, John, *The Race Race*. London: SCM Press, 1970.

Wirth, Louis, "The Problem of Minority Groups," Ralph Linton, ed., in *The Science of Man in the World Crisis*. New York: Columbia University Press, 1975.

Women's Division, Board of Global Ministries, The United Methodist Church, *A Charter for Racial Justice Policies in an Interdependent Global Community*. Board of Global Ministries, United Methodist Church, April 1978.

World Council of Churches, *The Uppsala Report*. Geneva: World Council of Churches, 1968.

Wright, Nathan, *Black Power and Urban Unrest*. New York: Hawthorn Books, 1967.

Zangwill, Israel, *The Melting Pot: Drama in Four Acts*, New York: Macmillan Co., 1921.